Finally, encouragement to think for ourselves! Marcia Ford has tapped into a major frustration for Christians who don't fit neatly into one political party or a label such as Conservative, Progressive, Moderate, etc. How many Christians would that be? In my estimation, practically all of us! This well-written and well-researched book is not only a breath of fresh air; it portends the winds of change to individualized politics.
—DR. JOEL C. HUNTER, senior pastor of Northland—A Church Distributed and author of *Right Wing, Wrong Bird: Why the Tactics of the Religious Right Won't Fly for Most Conservative Christians*

What a refreshing book! Marcia Ford has almost convinced me to give up my partisan political positions and join her. This book is fun, insightful, clear, and helpful. It may or may not change your views, but it will make you think. Then you will rise up and call Marcia Ford and me blessed. Her for writing it, and me for recommending it to you.
—STEVE BROWN, author, professor at Reformed Theological Seminary in Orlando, and president of the media ministry Key Life Network, Inc.

With a journalist's eye for accuracy and a believer's passion for truth, Marcia Ford lays bare the stubborn myth that in a nation divided by party allegiance, independent voters are aimless, apathetic, and irrelevant when it comes to the great issues of the day. *We the Purple* is a perceptive portrait of an awakening giant in a political system too often paralyzed by partisanship run amok. In frank, compelling, and sometimes irreverent prose, she offers a fresh vision of what it means to be people of faith in the public square.
—JEFFERY L. SHELER, contributing editor, *U.S. News & World Report,* and author of *Believers: A Journey into Evangelical America.*

In *We the Purple,* seasoned journalist Marcia Ford employs sass, spirituality, and statistics to expose the failings of our current two-party system that blocks independent voters from having a viable voice in the political arena. Using her piercing wit and keen research skills, she shines a light on both the failings of the Religious Right and the Progressive Left, when they align themselves with a given political party instead of following the teachings of the risen Christ. In particular, I pray that religious leaders will heed her clarion call to be pastors and preachers, not politicos.

—**BECKY GARRISON,** author of *Red and Blue God: Black and Blue Church*

We the PURPLE

★

FAITH, POLITICS, AND THE
INDEPENDENT VOTER

★

MARCIA FORD

TYNDALE HOUSE PUBLISHERS, INC.
CAROL STREAM, ILLINOIS

Visit Tyndale's exciting Web site at www.tyndale.com

Visit the author at her Web site: www.marciaford.com

TYNDALE and Tyndale's quill logo are registered trademarks of Tyndale House Publishers, Inc.

We the Purple: Faith, Politics, and the Independent Voter

Copyright © 2008 by Marcia Ford. All rights reserved.

Designed by Erik M. Peterson

Edited by Susan Taylor

Published in association with the literary agency of Alive Communications, Inc., 7680 Goddard Street, Suite 200, Colorado Springs, CO 80920.

Scripture quotations are taken from the Holy Bible, New International Version®. NIV®. Copyright © 1973, 1978, 1984 by International Bible Society. Used by permission of Zondervan. All rights reserved.

Library of Congress Cataloging-in-Publication

Ford, Marcia.
   We the purple : faith, politics, and the independent voter / Marcia Ford.
      p. cm.
   Includes bibliographical references.
   ISBN-13: 978-1-4143-1717-5 (hc)
   ISBN-10: 1-4143-1717-4 (hc)
   1. Christianity and politics—United States. 2. Party affiliation—United States.
3. Voting—United States. I. Title.
   JK2271.F67 2008
   324.973′0931—dc22   2007046707

Printed in the United States of America

14 13 12 11 10 09 08
 7   6   5   4   3   2   1

Lovingly and tolerantly dedicated to my husband, John, a committed nonvoter.

Contents

★

*We stand in the presence of an awakened nation,
impatient of partisan make-believe.*

★

WOODROW WILSON
1912 presidential campaign speech

Preface, or The Making of We the Purple

As RECENTLY AS FIVE YEARS AGO, the thought of writing—or reading—a political book would have made my stomach turn. To me, the word *politics* was synonymous with *partisan,* and I would have none of that.

But things change. I have long been a voter without a party, but for a long time I was also a Christian without a church. Several years ago, the blatant partisanship in some Christian communities left me on the outside, not even bothering to look in, so discouraging was the picture. But out there I discovered similarly dismayed, independent-minded believers (as well as independents of other faiths and no faith) who had grown tired of being labeled politically because of the church they attended. Their stories populate the pages that follow.

In addition to being a now-politically active independent voter, I'm also what some would call a seasoned journalist, which basically means I'm an old reporter. I thrive on research and one-on-one interviews, and *We the Purple* reflects those complementary passions that inform my professional life. I'm of the opinion that there's generally a 10 to 1 ratio between the amount of research material gathered and the amount that ends up in print. It doesn't matter to me whether that's a reasonable ratio or not. I'm a research junkie, and I don't care if 90 percent of my research just takes up space on my computer. All that is to assure you that much of what you'll read here is based on solid research. The rest is based on my generally unorthodox opinions and observations, but I'm confident you'll be able to make the distinction between legitimate research and personal blather.

Despite my commitment to journalistic objectivity, I started this project with the energy and gusto of a zealous standard-bearer for the independent cause. *I'll* show them, by golly—*I'll* show this country what independent voters are all about! We're not undecided! We're not easily swayed! We're not election spoilers! We're transforming the political process in America! That attitude lasted until, oh, a week or so after I signed the contract for *We the Purple*. In fact, I can tell you the exact time and date it expired: 10:10 a.m. on Tuesday, March 27, 2007, about ten minutes into a phone interview with John Dashler, who had attempted to run for governor of Georgia as an independent in 2006. That was the moment when Dashler began to describe the partisan machinations that tanked his campaign.

That was also the moment when I waded into the swampland that covers so much political territory. Independent voters like me are able to face an election with a fierce sense of optimism, but the manner in which independent and third-party candidates must face elections is another matter altogether. As you'll discover, some of these candidates are among the most courageous people you're likely to meet. It's no exaggeration to describe some of them as people who have pledged their "lives, [their] fortunes, and [their] sacred honor" in a relentless effort to bring about political reform.

Over the course of the next six months, I conducted dozens of interviews with independent voters and candidates, politicians, political observers, and activists of many stripes. By "stripes," I'm referring to both ideology and party affiliation. With regard to ideology, despite the perception that independents are mostly liberals, I've met and interviewed independents from one end of the ideological spectrum to the other. With regard to party affiliation, independents generally welcome into our big tent members and candidates of minor parties (so-called third parties), because the obstacles and issues that apply to us also pose challenges to them. Unfortunately, the reverse is not always the case; some minor parties have opposed independents' efforts to attain equal rights both as voters and as candidates. In any event, most often when I use the word *independent* I'm including minor parties in the discussion. The exceptions to that wider definition should be clear by the context.

A WORD ABOUT LABELS

Impossible. That's a word about labels.

Political labels, I've decided, are impossible to define. Just as soon as I come up with the perfect definition of a term like *centrist,* I can guarantee that someone will come along with some nitpicky argument designed to discredit me and thereby call into question the credibility of everything else I write, including the stories from my own life that I'm about to regale you with. If you don't believe it, pick a random political blog.[1] You'll find someone whose sole purpose in life is to dispute the incredibly trivial details of someone else's perspective. So take terms like *conservative, liberal, radical, moderate, centrist,* and the like with a healthy dose of salt. Please.

★

Acknowledgments

I have received more help on this one book than on all my previous books combined, so I can only hope that my memory and my notes have served me well in compiling this collection of names. I owe a tremendous debt of gratitude to each person below, as well as to countless others who maintain organizations, Web sites, and blogs that provide excellent information on and insight into political activity of every kind—independent, third-party, and even (gasp!) partisan.

I am most grateful to:

- Jackie Salit and the staff of the Committee for a Unified Independent Party (CUIP) and its Neo-Independent magazine: Nancy Ross, Fran Miller, Gwen Mandell, John Opdycke, Sarah Lyons, and CUIP co-founder Lenora Fulani, the first African-American and female presidential candidate to get on the ballot in all fifty states—as an independent, of course.

- Those who agreed to be interviewed and gave so generously of their time: Omar Ali; Jose Barrera; Lisa Braun; Mitch Campbell; David Cherry; Mike Clawson; Mike Crane; Linda Curtis; John Dashler; Craig Detweiler; Russ Diamond; Bob Friedman; Lenora Fulani; Nancy Hanks; Jerome Holden; John Koza; Richard Land; Emily Lewy; Joseph McCormick; Jonathan Merritt; Audrey Mowdy; Michael Ostrolenk;

Russ Ouellette; Larry Reinsch; Mark Ritter; Carl Romanelli; Kat Schrode; Maggy Simony; Mike Telesca; Suzi Wanga; Betty Ward; Richard Winger; and Robert B. Winn. Special thanks to Becky Garrison for providing valuable contact information.

- The entire Beers group at Tyndale House Publishers, particularly Carol Traver, Sue Taylor, and Maria Eriksen. They made this a better book than it otherwise would have been, and they made the entire process a delightful experience as well.

- My agent at Alive Communications, Beth Jusino, who picked up on my passion for nonpartisan politics and encouraged me to share that passion with you, the reading public. You can thank her for taking my idea for an essay and transforming it into a whole entire book that's thirty times longer than my original idea would have been.

★

Independents' Day, 11/7/2006

★

Together, the two parties function like giant down comforters, allowing the candidates to disappear into the enveloping softness, protecting them from exposure to the harsh weather of independent thought.
—Jon Stewart, Ben Karlin, or David Javerbaum[1]

Few days in the history of humankind have been as satisfying to independent thinkers as was November 7, 2006. Yes, I'm overstating things, but only to point out the political puffery that permeates the U.S. political system. Even *independents* are susceptible to this. Imagine that! Still, we know we affected the outcome of the election on November 7, 2006, and we have the stats to prove it. By the Election Day '06 midterms—a heady day for indie voters—we had found our voice and settled in to witness our contribution to history. The midterm results presaged what the nation can expect from the purple electorate in the run-up to the 2008 presidential election—which could spell trouble for any gloating Dems, because we're turning up the heat and holding their feet to the subsequent blazing flames.

But I'm getting ahead of myself.

TWO YEARS EARLIER

A warm and homey kitchen on a chilly fall evening, the savory aroma of a home-cooked meal, a half-dozen kindred spirits

alternately laughing and discussing the deeper issues of life—
how could it get any better than this? Relaxed and mellow and
grateful, I truly became immersed in the moment, in the *now,* a
highly unusual and blissful place for me to be. My other life, a
life I also love, was a mere 343.53 miles away from the contem-
plative Christian prayer center to which I had retreated three
days earlier. But it seemed much farther away, that other life
with all its stresses and annoyances and everydayness. This—this
quiet, secluded haven, this pocket of serenity—was a place where
I could slow down and pray and meditate and maybe even enter-
tain a profound thought or two.

But then, just as my facial muscles were about to form that
contented, amused smile that only Buddhists seem capable of
achieving, someone at the table—a traitor to the contempla-
tive cause, I later decided—*someone* said the dreaded "K" word.
Kerry. It was late October in 2004, and John Kerry had just committed another of his preelection gaffes. As if on cue, everyone
sighed a despairing sigh. *That Kerry. There he goes again. What
are we going to do with him?* "Well, I know it's not enough to
keep us from voting for him," said the thief who had just made
off with my peace, "but still . . ."

As her voice trailed off, I bristled, no doubt perceptibly. What
did she mean, "us"? How could this stranger possibly know
whether I was a Kerry supporter—or if I was, how much it
would take for me to change my mind about him? That led to a
scarier question: Did my presence at this particular prayer center
peg me as a . . . a *Democrat?* And an equally scary question: If I
objected to her assumption, however graciously, would everyone
mentally label me a . . . a *Republican?*

I kept silent. This was not the time or the place for political dispute. The director of the center, bless her peacemaking
heart, gently got us back on track. We had intentionally broken

silence during supper, and now we would return to silence. As relieved as I was that our conversation had ended, I couldn't shake the feeling—the reality—that once again, I didn't fit in with my brothers and sisters in Christ. And all because of partisan politics.

The truth is, I am every partisan politician's worst nightmare—a registered independent. Wildly unpredictable in my voting habits over the last three decades and more, I have cast ballots for Democrats, Republicans, independents, and assorted loose cannons. I have also cast ballots *against* Democrats, Republicans, independents, and assorted loose cannons. And I have cast no ballot at all in those years when political ennui overtook me, when voting for the lesser of two evils appeared to be more evil than not voting at all. In those years, I intentionally avoided the evil of two lessers.

People like me have come to be known as purple voters—neither Republican red nor Democratic blue—thanks to Massachusetts congressman Barney Frank. At a 2002 bipartisan press conference promoting a bill to legalize the medical use of marijuana, Frank, a Democrat, said this: "I even noted, by the way, we do believe this ought to appeal both to Democrats, Republicans, liberals and conservatives. You notice we have a new color scheme here. We have green states and white states. But I would point out that the green states are composed of both red states and blue states." (At this point, Frank is interrupted by laughter.) "Now, that may be a color combination that you don't get from the spectrum. I guess—what?—red and blue will give you purple states."[2] Since then, Frank's reference to "purple states" has led to the use of the term *purple voters,* which gradually made its way into the political lexicon. But in 2004, it had yet to make its way into my consciousness.

As I walked back to the sanctuary of my private room at the

retreat center, I wondered if I would ever meet another nonpartisan Christian. The leadership of my own church was clearly Republican, though they took care not to declare that from the pulpit. Still, their affiliation was so evident and the sermons were so politically tainted that I had quit attending the misnamed "worship" services several months earlier when the election season began to heat up. The situation was even worse at another church where I was part of a small group; there, the congregation was split down the middle along partisan lines, and the rancor between the two groups was tangible.

I was not only a voter without a party; I was also a Christian without a church.

MUSINGS: NOVEMBER 7, 2006

What a difference two years can make. Today I felt as if I was part of a vast, invisible army of nonpartisan voters trooping off to make history. By all accounts, we're the ones who will tip the scales in this election. But right now I'm content to sit and knit, satisfied that earlier today I voted according to my conscience—and for the first time, I didn't feel alone in that activity. Over the years I've known lots of Democrats, lots of Republicans, lots of nonvoters, and a Libertarian or two, but finally—*finally!*—I know more than a few independents. We call ourselves by different names, some preferring *nonpartisans,* others opting for *centrists* or *moderates* or *radicals,* still others—like me—enchanted with *purple voters,* and almost all disdaining the term *swing voters,* but we share this in common: We swear allegiance to no political party.

That, of course, makes us the enemies of the partisan segment of the electorate. A very good and very Democratic friend of mine once got right in my face and blamed me for George W. Bush's re-election in 2004. I never felt so powerful in all my life.

Me! Single-handedly deciding a presidential election simply by filling in a not-Kerry, not-Bush circle! (We hadn't gone Diebold yet in my voting district. In fact, we still haven't.)

By now, I've heard all the criticism that's leveled at independents: Our votes are wasted, we're wishy-washy, we have no convictions, we can't make up our minds. None of which is true, but there you go. On this day, that criticism rolls right off my back; I know how important our vote—my vote—is to this year's midterm candidates, especially GOP incumbents. If nothing else, the political chatter for months has underscored this one point: Neither major party can afford to dismiss purple voters as irrelevant.

Tonight I'll forgo network television, with its "up-to-the-minute, you-heard-it-first-here!" breaking election news. I'll get all the political news I need at 11 p.m. Eastern, when Jon Stewart and Stephen Colbert have promised a full hour of election coverage on Comedy Central. Of course, if this election follows the pattern of elections in recent years, we won't know the results of some of the major contests until tomorrow or later anyway. Tomorrow's soon enough. Right now, I'm basking in the delicious feeling that today, I made a difference. I do believe I have not felt this politically content since I cast my first vote in 1972. So McGovern got walloped that year, but I *voted*. Casting my ballot never felt quite that good in subsequent elections. Until this year, that is, when my ballot sealed my identity as a purple voter.

THE MORNING AFTER

You might think that independents across the land woke up on November 8, 2006 in a universal state of near-euphoria. Some did, of course. This was the year when we would make our voices heard by bringing about *change,* and there's certainly something intoxicating about knowing that our votes made a difference in the outcome of the election and in the very balance of power on a congressional level.

But here's where the nuances of purple thinking enter the picture. And here's where I have to switch from writing about "we" to writing about me—because independents, being so, well, independent, don't think alike. My reaction to the midterm results went like this: I was glad that the balance of power shifted; the party in power on November 7 had for years displayed an unconscionable measure of arrogance, and they needed to be ousted. But was I euphoric that it was the Democrats who clearly won the day? Not really. Bear in mind that to me, the fact that the lawmakers who needed to be voted out were all Republicans and that those who would take their seats were Democrats was purely a technicality. As a nonpartisan voter, I would just as passionately vote out members of the Democratic or Reform or Libertarian or Green parties—or even an independent—if they ever betrayed my trust to the extent that the Bush administration has—but there I'm getting ahead of myself again.

What I'm saying is that independents like me intend to keep the Democrats' feet to the fire. We have no allegiance to the party, no partisan ideology to uphold, no reason to ever vote for them again if they don't do something to fix what needs fixing. I have a list of what needs fixing, by the way, starting with the war in Iraq. My list is a pretty long one, but first things first.

HOPE, FAITH, AND THE POLITICAL PROCESS

One Christian political activist that I respect—though I don't always agree with him—is Jim Wallis, founder and editor of *Sojourners* magazine and author of *God's Politics: Why the Right Gets It Wrong and the Left Doesn't Get It.* Following the '06 midterms, Wallis, who has long been critical of the religious right, told the *Philadelphia Inquirer* that he believed the Christian vote should always be "up for grabs"; if Christians voted according to their beliefs, then no party could own them. "The religious vote should always be a swing vote," Wallis said. "We should be morally centered but not centrists; religion should play a prophetic role."[3]

If religion is to play a prophetic role in the culture and in the political process, then people of faith need the freedom to speak prophetic words openly, without fear of repercussion or losing face. As a religion journalist, I personally know many Christian leaders who are so closely aligned with either of the two major parties that they will dig their heels in and defend the actions of their party's politicians even when those actions are contrary to what they themselves believe and know to be morally and ethically right. I understand why they do this, though I wish I didn't. I wish I could remain oblivious, scratch my head, and go through life wondering what on earth they were thinking. But their reasons are clear: They don't want their ministries to lose the support of the party faithful, and they don't want to suffer the embarrassment of publicly admitting they were wrong. Wallis is right; as paradoxical as the image may seem, if Christians remained morally centered, their votes could swing all along the political spectrum. And that includes the votes of prominent Christian leaders.

Mind you, I have no quarrel with those conservative or liberal or radical or reactionary Christians who consistently vote according to their consciences. It would be really nice if they would return the favor and not quarrel with me when I vote according to my unaffiliated conscience, but so be it. I just won't bicker in return. I know we're far closer in our beliefs than we may appear to be to the untrained eye. I just happened to have trained my eye to focus on our points of agreement.

And that has led me to the conviction that we're nowhere near as polarized as the political talking heads would have us believe we are. Let's face it; it's to the partisan politicians' advantage to convince us that we're so far apart on the major political issues that we simply *have* to pledge our allegiance to the party whose platform lines up with our perspectives. Maybe it's just me— maybe I'm unusually blessed—but most of the people I know are pretty reasonable, whether they realize it or not. Whenever I'm able to talk them down off their partisan ledges and engage them in a sensible discussion about the very real problems in our society, more often than not I find that at some point a light clicks on, and even they have to admit that they're not as committed to the party line as they thought they were.

Yes, there are some black-and-white issues in life, but there's a whole lot of gray out there as well. And yes, there are red and blue voters in America, but there are a whole lot of purple voters as well. In the following pages, you'll find out just who these voters are and how they're quietly shaking up the political landscape. I say "quietly" because although we can be a raucous bunch, we're not prone to public displays of political fervor. As Jon Stewart, host of *The Daily Show* on Comedy Central, once said, punching the air with his fist: "It's not like we're going to take to the streets and shout, 'Be reasonable!'" But keep that image in your head as you continue to read—the image of a powerful group of independent voters with their metaphorical fists in the air, mentally shouting, "Be reasonable!"

Marcia Ford

★

Chapter One

Purple Reign

★

*Purples like me have their work cut out for them,
if we are to serve as any kind of meaningful bridge
across the cultural divide.*
—Marlowe C. Embree, Ph.D.
  Social psychologist

am a Christian, and what's more, a Christian with one foot planted in the evangelical world and the other in a more inclusive faith community. Politically, I am neither red nor blue. I don't vote solely on a candidate's stand on one particular issue. I'm far more complex than that, and that makes me what has come to be known as a purple voter. And you know what? There are a lot of people, even people of faith—even *evangelicals!*—who are just like me.

I've met independent voters who take their faith seriously. Most of them are Christians and Jews, though I'm sure there's a contingent of Islamic independent voters that I've yet to discover. And I've met many Buddhists, as well as people who express faith in the universe, or in an overriding moral law, or in the human spirit, who are also independent voters or members of minor parties, also known as third parties.

I've met independent voters whose political views span the entire ideological spectrum, from ultraconservative to ultraliberal. Some are antiabortion, others proabortion. Some support the war in Iraq; others oppose it. Some oppose gay marriage;

some support it, and still others don't care one way or another about what they consider to be a nonissue. The independent voters I engage with on a regular basis are impossible to pigeonhole.

As diverse as we are, we do share one nearly universal concern: the need for political reform. *Major* political reform. *Radical* political reform. The kind of reform that takes the axe to the root of the problem—the problem being partisanship run amok.

We're a frustrated lot, we purple voters. Disenchanted by candidates and incumbents on both sides of the political aisle, we're looking for leaders who are committed to working together to solve problems instead of digging in their heels on the party line. Our discontent has led to the phenomenal growth in the number of independent voters among the U.S. electorate, a segment estimated to make up as much as 42 percent of actual voters nationwide following the 2006 midterm elections. Despite that percentage, politicians have until recently paid little attention to our concerns. They wanted our vote but not our input. They saw us as swing voters who could be enticed to their side of the political divide. Because we're generally not strident activists who make our presence known all over the map, they considered us important only in the so-called swing states. They were wrong, and the '06 midterms proved it.

Six years earlier—from my then-home in Florida, of all places—I witnessed firsthand the debacle that was the 2000 presidential election, reported on it for *Charisma Online* e-newsletter, yawned my way through the '02 midterms, fumed over the absence of a write-in option for president on my precinct's '04 ballot, and tried ever so hard to contain my temptation to gloat after the 2006 rout—especially over the number of candidates and voters who pledged to turn independent the following day. (I should note that I did not watch any election coverage

on Election Day '06 until Comedy Central's live coverage late
that night, for the same reason that I faithfully avoid watching
the Sunday morning political shouting matches: I value my sanity.) My adamantly nonpolitical husband, John, tolerates the fact
that I actually vote more often than not. Our two young-adult
daughters wish I'd vote a straight Democratic ticket, but I figure
they're still young. They'll come around eventually.

Those six years found me in something of a political incuba-
tor. I had spent a half-century in the safe and secure womb of
the politically uninvolved. In the aftermath of the 2000 presidential election, I emerged from that sheltered environment not
so much because of who was elected but because of how he was
elected. I could see—anyone could see—that there was something fundamentally wrong with our electoral system, but I saw
no hope of it changing in my lifetime. For the next six years I
continued to go quietly about my long-standing independent
ways. Something was growing inside me. I can now call what it
was—a sense of utter outrage—but like a preemie in an incuba-
tor, I didn't have the capacity to raise a loud cry.

I still don't. I am not and never have been a strident, take-to-
the-streets-in-protest kind of person—not in the antiwar '60s,
the feminist '70s, the—um—what exactly was it that we were
protesting in the '80s and '90s? But in 2006, I found my voice,
my political voice. I won't raise that voice in the streets, but I'll
wear out this keyboard and my fingertips writing about it in
that voice.

THE COLOR PURPLE

I have always loved the color purple. I'm guessing that has
something to do with two distinct factors from my distant past:
flannelgraphs and hippies.[1] Anyone who has missed out on the
richness of a genuine faith experience has indeed suffered a great

misfortune, but those who have missed out on the joys of the Sunday school flannelgraph are to be pitied the most. In the mainline Protestant world of my childhood, a flannelgraph represented the best the church had to offer: brightly colored biblical figures that would quietly find their places on an equally colorful background depicting the Temple in Jerusalem or the shoreline of Galilee or a humble home in Bethany that nevertheless looked a whole lot better than my own. Then there were the miniature pieces that lent authenticity to the scene: baskets of loaves and fishes, jugs of water that would soon turn to wine, fishing boats that sailed on a turbulent sea.

The scenes depicting royalty were among my favorites. How could you not love the image of Queen Esther, draped in a purple robe that symbolized her royal status, placing her life on the line before her husband, the king? Oh, the drama! The tension! The purple!

It's not surprising that decades later, I invested money—an amount we couldn't afford to invest—in a complete set of flannelgraph figures and scenes and accessories, along with a full-size flannel board. Full-sized video screens had replaced full-sized flannel boards by the time my children came of Sunday school age in the 1980s, but I was not about to have them miss out on this exquisite experience.

Even before that, quite by accident I discovered what purple, and its pastel kin, lavender, could do for my appearance, which needed doing for. In my hippie heyday, I bought a new pair of prescription glasses with lavender frames and lavender-tinted lenses, mainly because I thought they were ultrahip. But a couple of weird things happened: Friends started noticing the color of my eyes and stopped telling me how tired I looked all the time. It seems the tinted lenses brought out the green in my otherwise hazel eyes and diminished the appearance of the genetically induced dark circles under my eyes. Trust me, I would have worn plaid every day for the rest of my life if I thought it would stop thoughtless people from saying, "Oh, you look so tired!" I'm just grateful that it was the colors of the purple spectrum that did the trick and not a chartreuse plaid-and-stripe ensemble.

The love of purple never left me. For decades thereafter I was purple when purple wasn't cool.

These days, at least politically, purple is the new cool, in part because of a freshman computer-programming project at Princeton University in 2000 directed by Dr. Robert Vanderbei, chair of Princeton's Operations Research and Financial Engineering Department.[2] Vanderbei felt that the traditional maps showing red and blue states did not accurately reflect voting results and that a detailed map of a county-by-county tally, showing regions that were a mix of Republican and Democratic votes, would reveal that the country is nowhere near as polarized as the media and partisan politicians would have us believe.

The resulting "Purple America" map made Vanderbei the equivalent of a rock star among political junkies.[3] Since then, Vanderbei has created similar maps for subsequent presidential elections and one very cool interactive map that shows the purple-ization of America from 1960 to 2004.[4] Independent and third-party voters should find the interactive map particularly interesting, as it clearly shows, in green, the counties that helped give George Wallace 13 percent of the popular vote and an impressive 46 electoral college votes in 1968 and Ross Perot 19 percent of the popular vote (and no electoral college votes) in 1992.

Writing in the April 24, 2006, issue of *New York* magazine, Kurt Andersen offers up an intriguing idea: Why not start a Purple Party?[5] I'm not what you'd call a party person these days, but if I ever were to join a political party (oh, my; what would it take?), I'd naturally gravitate toward a purple one. Here's part of Andersen's premise: "Less than a third of the electorate are happy to call themselves Republicans, and only a bit more say they're Democrats—but between 33 and 39 percent now consider themselves neither Democrat nor Republican. In other words, there are more of us than there are of either of them."[6]

Andersen wants moderates to abandon the baggage of the two major parties and create a "serious, innovative, truth-telling, pragmatic" third party that would field candidates who are capable not only of winning but also of governing—a party of "passionately practical progressives" who represent the middle. The time, he says, is right, given that in 1992 independent candidate Ross Perot—you really have to read the entire article, if only for his description of Perot—received more votes than the incumbent president, George H. W. Bush, in Maine, and Bill Clinton in Utah.

And Andersen suggests launching the Purple Party in New York City, writing:

> For a generation now this city's governance has tended to be strikingly moderate, highly flexible rather than ideological or doctrinaire. . . . For 24 of the past 28 years the mayors we have elected—Koch, Giuliani, Bloomberg—have been emphatically independent-minded moderates whose official party labels have been flags of convenience. . . . We're certainly not part of red-state America, but when push comes to shove we are really not blue in the D.C.–Cambridge–Berkeley–Santa Monica sense. We are, instead, like so much of the country, vividly purple.[7]

There you have it. Now that I've made the case for purple voters, though, I need to fess up, issue one of my many disclaimers, and beg your indulgence. Because the truth is, many independents, myself included, technically aren't purple voters at all. True purple voters are a mix of red and blue. We, however, are often considered to be more like muddy voters. We may vote red or blue, but we are also likely to vote neither. If we vote for the Green Party, that really muddies the red and blue waters. Actually, I prefer to think of us as crystal-clear voters. We're far more clear on *what* we want and *who* we want than politicians seem to realize.

SO WHO ARE WE . . . AND WHAT DO WE WANT?

For starters, independent voters represent at least a third of the electorate and possibly as much as 42 percent, depending on which poll you read. Let's go with the lower number so I'll appear to be objective, even though I'm not. That figure comes to us compliments of the Rasmussen Reports, "The Best Place to Look for Polls That Are Spot On."[8] Rasmussen's spot-on poll of 15,000 American adults taken in May 2007 showed a decline in the number of people who self-identified as either Republican (30.8 percent, down from a peak of 37.8 percent in 2004) or Democrat (36.3 percent, down from 38 percent just six months earlier, right after the 2006 rout).

Which means, of course, that those who self-identify as independents or "unaffiliated" took up the slack, polling at what Rasmussen calls an "all-time high" of 32.9 percent—more than the percentage of Republicans. To put that in perspective, as recently as 1988 only 10 percent of registered voters considered themselves to be independents.

Ideologically, we run the gamut from right-wing fundies to radical lefties, from proabortion conservatives to anti-gay marriage liberals, from embarrassed ex-Republicans to disillusioned ex-Democrats, from Catholic, mainline Protestant, and evangelical Christians to religious and secular Jews to Buddhists and the ever popular "highly spiritual" types. And speaking of evangelicals, I can't think of another group that has benefited more from the growing respectability that independents are enjoying. Switching to an independent voting status has given many an evangelical permission to safely jump the *U.S.S. GOP* without having to board the foundering, and floundering, Democratic ship. Unless you've been there, you have no idea how much pressure there is on lay leaders in particular to toe the party line—and how much courage it takes to buck the evangelical and fundamentalist religious systems (they are not identical, by the way).

Theodore Roosevelt was the first person to use the term *bully pulpit* to describe the presidency as a place of extraordinary influence, without the pejorative connotation we attach to the word *bully* today or the literal, religious association of the word *pulpit*. But let me attach and associate both, because the pejorative and literal meanings *do* apply to some of today's conservative churches and religious organizations and, on occasion, to the presidency.

One misused and abused Bible verse has led to the contemporary use of the bully pulpit. That verse is found in Matthew 12:30 in the New International Version: "He who is not with me is against me." That's Jesus speaking, and in the context, he has just healed a demon-possessed man. The religious leaders of the day—which Jesus so eloquently calls a "brood of vipers"—deny his wonder-working powers, so in Matthew 12:30 he's basically telling them off.

Well, I'd say anyone who has just exorcised a demon has that right, Jesus foremost among them, since he did it more than once. But when you take his words out of context and begin broadly applying them to your own domain, you're on shaky ground. Those of us with evangelical ears knew exactly what President Bush meant shortly after 9/11 when he said,

"You're either with us or against us in the fight against terror." Bush knows his Bible, and he knew those words would resonate with an evangelical base that knows the Bible just as well. They had likely heard their own pastors use that verse to get the congregation to line up behind their own interpretations of the Bible—or their own political persuasions. I even know of at least one large Christian company that tried to use the verse to weed out any employees who did not toe the corporate-religious line.

But many evangelicals and conservatives have reached what I call a "Hold it!" moment. Hold it—what right do these people have to use the words of Jesus to keep me in lockstep with them? Hold it—what makes them think they have divine, supernatural powers? Hold it—what does it mean to be "with us"?

A growing discomfort with the church's alignment with the Republican Party, coupled with a refreshing freedom to question the authority of our old-guard leaders, has awakened many evangelicals to the ramifications of that lockstep obedience. And that means they finally feel free of the pressure to conform to conservative religious Republican voting patterns and party allegiance—which is what led us down this five-paragraph sidetrack to begin with.

The original point was that independent voters cannot be neatly categorized. There are some things we all agree on, like the need to change the political system, but we are hardly on the same ideological page. Let me take a stab, though, at clearing up some misconceptions and maybe providing a clearer picture of who independents are. Here are *some* characteristics of *some* of us:

- We're tired—tired of two parties whose main priority is self-preservation and self-promotion rather than serving the people who voted them into office.

- We have no problem voting for someone who has absolutely no chance of winning.
- We vote for the person and not the party.
- We wouldn't vote a straight, major-party ticket if they paid us to, which I have no doubt they will try to do at some point.[9]
- We are not *un*decided. We have *decided* to be independent.
- We believe that a diversity of opinions stimulates healthy debate.
- We believe that the two major parties suppress a diversity of opinions and stifle healthy debate.
- We want dialogue, not diatribes.
- Sometime before we die, we'd like the warm-and-fuzzy experience of a government that follows the will of the people instead of one that manipulates it.
- We care as much about what happens on the remaining 364 days of the year as we do about what happens on Election Day. And about how it happens.[10]
- We *want* Ralph Nader to keep on running and keep on fighting and keep on debating, even if we don't vote for him. We probably need to apologize for that.
- We're inconsistent. We are antiparty, and yet we welcome all third-party voters and candidates to join us under the independent umbrella.
- Maybe we're not that inconsistent. We're outsiders, and we welcome all other outsiders to join us. There, that's better.
- We thank God for creating the Internet just so he could bring independents together, except for the atheists among us, who probably thank Al Gore.[11]
- We believe the United States is better than this.[12]

FEELING ALL ALONE?

As I talked with independents across the nation, I discovered that I was not alone in what I had thought was an unorthodox way of thinking about politics. What I also discovered is that I was not alone in feeling alone. Time after time I heard some variation on this sentiment: "I didn't know there was anyone else out there who felt the way I did about the two major parties. I considered myself to be independent, but then I kept hearing independent voters referred to as 'undecideds.' But that didn't describe me, so I wasn't sure what I was, other than maybe a political anomaly."

Maybe we are a political anomaly. Even so, there are more independents out there than most of us realize, especially if we hesitate to express our own political views in an environment where doing so is likely to incite conflict or rancor. We don't know any other independents because we don't talk about our own independent voting habits in, say, a church that clearly considers it a sin to not vote for a Republican, or in a close-knit, extended family that has voted for Democrats as long as there have been Democrats. Which is one reason why I believe God invented the Internet, but more on that later.

Meanwhile, let's look at how many independents there are and at how their numbers are growing, in a random sample of U.S. states. Bear in mind that the terminology varies from one state to another (e.g., "no party" or "decline to state"), but for our purposes here I'm designating all those who are neither Democrats nor Republicans as independents:

- **Arizona:** In the past decade, almost 300,000 voters have registered as independent, nearly doubling in number to 712,765, or 27 percent of the state's 2.6 million voters—a significant percentage in a traditionally Republican state.

- **California:** If recent trends continue, independents may outnumber Republicans and Democrats within the next two decades. More than 1 million of the state's 3 million independents have been added to the voter registration rolls in just eight years.[13]

- **Colorado:** The number of independent voters increased in suburban Denver between 2004 and 2006, while the numbers of Republican voters declined and Democratic voters held steady. The percentage of increase in independents in just four counties ranged from 32.8 percent to 36 percent, according to the *Rocky Mountain News,* which pointed out that the 2 million potential voters in the Denver suburbs generally determine the outcome of elections.[14]

- **Florida:** Of the state's 2 million independent voters, 680,000 registered in the last decade. Democratic registration has dropped by nearly a half million voters; Republican registration has also declined.[15]

- **Iowa:** Some 39 percent of the state's 2 million voters are registered as independents in a state that can make or break a candidate early on.

- **Maine:** Data from the 2006 election indicates that 38 percent of voters registered as independent or third-party voters; Green Party registrants were tabulated separately, at 3 percent, bringing the actual total to 41 percent. That compares with Democrats at 31 percent and Republicans at 28 percent.

- **New Hampshire:** In the past decade, the number of independents has grown by 62 percent. They now represent 44 percent of registered voters.[16] About 85 percent of first-time registrants have declined to register as members of either major party.

- **Pennsylvania:** The state's nearly 1 million independent voters represent about 12 percent of all registered voters, but that's a whopping 257 percent increase in just ten years.[17]

If your state isn't listed—this really is a random sampling, with other dramatic stats to be found in other states—you should be able to get them from your secretary of state's office or on its Web site under "elections" or a similar designation. Some states make it fairly easy to find the voter registration data you're looking for online, while others make you jump through an untold number of cyberhoops before you realize they just don't want to accommodate you. Simply another reason to vote for someone who *will* accommodate the citizenry.

And independent voters do expect to be accommodated.

WE WON'T BE *IGNORED*

In an insightful "I told you so" article in the *Weekly Standard*—appropriately titled "You Gotta Be Purple to Win"—John J. DiIulio Jr. shared this bit of wisdom with his fellow Democrats two weeks after the 2006 midterms:

> You can't effectively court a purple-voter majority with faux-purple candidates, or wait to show your purple colors till the election is all but over. Real purple Democrats won even in many states and districts where both the president and Republican incumbents were not as wildly unpopular as they were in Philadelphia and its suburbs.
>
> Attentive purple voters will be listening and watching. If the Democrats' leaders in Congress slip into ultraliberal attack mode, then they will be rebuked, and the whole party will suffer.[18]

Two years earlier, DiIulio had warned the Democrats that they needed to "start winning and stop whining by wooing America's purple . . . majority."[19] After the Democrats took control of Congress, he warned them that if they didn't start helping President Bush lead the country, especially with regard to Iraq, then their candidates, "purple or not, will lose in 2008, and deservedly so." This is the same John J. DiIulio, by the way, who served as the first director of the White House Office of Faith-Based and Community Initiatives. He understands purple thinking, particularly from a faith perspective. At this writing, in the summer of 2007, his second warning is, as our friends at Rasmussen would say, spot-on.

However brilliant DiIulio's advice may be—independents everywhere would positively swoon if the Democrats would actually help Bush lead the country—no Democrat in his or her right mind will ever heed it. Because that would mean taking the high road, and neither party will abide that. So instead, the citizenry has to suffer through another insufferable round of the blame game. No wonder so many Americans throw their arms up in despair and turn down the opportunity to participate in the political process by casting a vote. Just writing this makes me want to avoid voting, and *I'm* a borderline political activist.

Which brings up another issue: not voting. I don't expect to get a whole lot of support on this, from independents or anyone else, but I respect a person's decision not to vote. I'm not even sure I care *why* they choose not to vote. Maybe it's for a noble reason, like they cannot in good conscience vote for any of the candidates or any of the ballot issues. Or maybe it's for a somewhat less noble reason, like they have no idea what's going on and they don't want to taint the electoral process with their ignorance. Or maybe it's for a completely ignoble reason, like they are just plain lazy and they care not a whit about their fellow man or woman. Here's why I defend their right not to vote: because I hate "get out the vote" messages.

You know the ones. Suddenly there's Rory Gilmore—Alexis Bledel—filling up your television screen, awkwardly chiding you: "If you don't vote, you lose your right to complain." Every time I saw one of those public service announcements, I wanted to fire back, "Oh yeah?" And I was a voter! Still, I was highly offended. The way I figure it, no one—*no one*—has the right to take away my right to complain, whether I vote or not. Not Rory, not Alexis, not anyone. So my nose got all out of joint, and I started defending the right of nonvoters to complain. No one listened, but I stand by that defense. Remember, I'm all about the freedom. In this case, the freedom of speech.

This is a book about voters, though, so I'll leave those nonvoters to their beer and potato chips and complaining ways. (It works both ways. I'm also free to be judgmental.)

Let me give you just one example of what happens when politicians take our calls. This happened in New Hampshire, whose citizens live free or die. As we just learned, it's home to a large percentage of independent voters, some 44 percent of the electorate. It's also home to the nation's first presidential primary every four years. And it's home to some of the country's most independent and active independent activists.

I would not want to be on the opposing side of an issue supported by the New Hampshire Committee for an Independent Voice (NH-CIV).

Cofounded by fourth-grade school teacher Betty Ward and lawyer André Gibeau, the group was organized in part to fight a 2005 bill that would have required the state's independents—who are allowed to vote in primaries if they register with a party on the day of the primary—to wait ninety days to regain their status as independents (officially identified, to their consternation, as "undeclared" in New Hampshire). As independents saw it, they were being forced to remain a member of a party against their will. They argued that if the bill passed, it would have the effect of discouraging voter participation in the primaries—and it would get candidates off the hook from talking to, and listening to, all the state's voters, not just party members. NH-CIV rallied independents to write, call, and e-mail their representatives and express their opposition to the bill, which was eventually killed in the state senate. They won that round, but then an identical bill resurfaced in 2006.

Well! That infuriated the state's independents, and you don't want to do that to 44 percent of the electorate if you hope to have any chance of being reelected someday. This time, they garnered nationwide support by enlisting independent voter organizations across the country to contact friends, family, and colleagues in New Hampshire to let them know about the bill and what they could do to defeat it. Voters in New Hampshire, most of them independents, bombarded their legislators with one clear message: Defeat this bill, or we'll hold you accountable in the next election.

Trust me, the independent voters in New Hampshire won't be *ignored*, and now their legislators know it.

ALL POLITICS IS LOCAL . . . SORT OF

As much as anyone, independent voters and candidates under-stand the truth in former House Speaker Tip O'Neill's comment that "all politics is local"—a bit of wisdom his father handed down to him. In an article unrelated to independent voting, environmental activist Thomas Kostigen gives us this visual image of the importance of local, grassroots activity: "That's why it's so important to enact local policy change. Policies, like hot air, rise. Enough local policy changes and soon national policymakers then international policymakers—in this case President Bush—will wake up and see the urgent need and cry for world-wide carbon-emission reductions."[20]

Now I'm not suggesting that we independents are blowing hot air, but I do like the image of local policies rising to national and international levels. We saw a bit of that in the New Hampshire battles over the open-primary law in 2005 and 2006. Make no mistake about it—this local issue attracted the attention of legislatures across the country. They were looking to see how the issue played out in one pivotal state, since other states were considering changing their own voting laws—this, thanks to a partisan effort to combat widespread voter fraud. Such fraud is so widespread, it seems, that it has virtually dissipated into the ozone, since no one has yet to produce one shred of evidence that voter integrity is in peril.

One of the best gifts independent voters can give their local communities, in addition to independent candidates, is a grassroots effort to establish nonpartisan elections on the municipal level. Most large cities, including Chicago and Los Angeles, already have nonpartisan elections, as do 80 percent of cities with populations of 200,000 or more. Smaller towns also need this reform, which would inject some life into a stagnant political climate. Remember this principle: Any time you eliminate partisanship, you improve the political climate. Okay, maybe that's not always true, but I don't know of a time that it's failed. What happens when you subtract partisanship? You get a much more vibrant field of candidates, including the occasional dunderhead who just might belong to one of those major parties anyway. You also get a livelier debate on whatever issues your community is facing. When a candidate is not beholden to a major political party, that candidate is free not only to speak her mind but also to engage in more creative problem-solving.

One of the rallying cries of the 1960s was "power to the people," and protestors have used it ever since to voice their opposition to what, back in the day, we called The Establishment. Now that we *are* The Establishment (*Can it really be true?*), respectable people like you and me can pick up that mantra again and make it all respectable-like by applying it to local elections. No, we don't need to do that "take to the streets and punch our fists in the air" thing that I mentioned earlier. Slogans in that context distort the meaning of genuine power in a democracy (or a republic, for you purists); we're not talking about a hostile takeover here. We're talking about the legitimate power granted to us in the Constitution, and we can regain it by strategically and lawfully removing it from the hands of the two major parties. To some people, I'm sure, that sounds like a no-brainer, to others, an impossibility, and to still others, an example of sophomoric idealism.[21]

Call it what you will, it can work on the local level.

SUCCESS IN THE CITY

Waterbury, Connecticut, is a city of just over a hundred thousand people and the place where my parents spent their honeymoon back in the late 1940s. I remember passing through there once and wondering why on earth they chose to honeymoon there. It's too late to ask them, so I just have to figure that the city held some kind of appeal for them back then. Today, it's a hotbed of independent political activity, a city that offers proof of the power of grassroots activism.

One thing you should know about Waterbury is that it's governed by a fifteen-member board of aldermen, who will probably be known someday as alderpersons or just plain alders. According to the city's at-large election law, each party is allowed to put up a slate of nine candidates. Did you get that? "Each party," meaning Democrats and Republicans. And did you get this? Eighteen candidates, fifteen seats. You've got to feel sorry for the three losers in a race like that. "If you don't like what's going on with the board of aldermen, the best you can do is un-elect three of them," Mike Telesca, who founded the city's Independent Party and serves as its chairman, told me in a 2007 interview.

In 2001, Telesca and other independents decided to challenge the system. Three independent candidates won seats on the board of aldermen, but they were denied the opportunity to serve. Why? "They said, 'Well, you're still Democrats. It doesn't matter that you didn't run with the party,'" Telesca continued. "So they gave our seats to the Republicans, even though we got more votes than they did."

Not surprisingly, the independent candidates took the matter to court. The court decided the city's charter did not adequately address the situation and instead based its decision on state law, which says that in at-large elections, no single party may hold more than two-thirds of the seats on the board. In Waterbury, that translates into ten seats. Well, the Democrats had come by the first nine seats honestly, one presumes, through the normal voting procedure, so the court decided the independents—who were Democrats in disguise, of course—should be allowed one seat, which was awarded to the independent candidate who received the most votes. Though the independents wanted to appeal, they knew the $25,000 or more needed for an appeal would be hard, if not impossible, to come by.

They dropped the court case, but they did not give up. In 2003, they formed the Independent Party, proving that they were not Democrats. That year, the Republicans all but gave up; nine Democratic candidates were elected, as were six independents. In that same election, two independents won four-year terms on the board of education; a third independent member was added in 2005, when another seat opened up. Telesca and his independent colleagues had broken Waterbury's two-party stranglehold, or actually, the one-party-with-two-names stranglehold.

"The coalition between Democrats and Republicans is so pervasive in this particular town that we have quite a history of corruption," Telesca added, explaining the Republicans' 2003 action—or rather, inaction. "The last two Republican mayors went to jail. In 2001 the mayor that was in office was taken out of his office in handcuffs. The Republicans at that point knew they couldn't win."[22]

What's most interesting about this is that the Independent Party had already been planning to put up a full slate of candidates in 2003 before the Republicans essentially dropped out. By creating an independent coalition to prove they were independents and not Democrats, they were able to take advantage of a future situation and fill the void left by the faltering Republicans.

It's seldom easy, but independents can begin to reform the political system by starting in their own municipalities. Waterbury is but one example of a city in which independents are beginning to clean up a corrupt political system.

Maybe that's the most accurate image of independents: We're the cleaner-uppers. Whatever action we take, our basic motivation is to clean things up—to sweep career politicians out of office, wipe out political corruption, clear away the clutter in the electoral system, and overhaul the two-party system. Yes, that image works for me.

PROFILE OF AN INDEPENDENT VOTER

Audrey Mowdy, 49, Conyers, Georgia

IN HER WORK as president and CEO of Rose of Sharon International Resource Center, Audrey Mowdy discovered what she calls "the most independent group there is"—the homeless and poverty-stricken people her organization serves. As it became clearer that this group was greatly impacted by public policy but had no voice in the process of developing that policy, she and others in the Atlanta area founded a political organization called iMove. Mowdy, an African-American and mother of two adult daughters, also serves as chairman of the Atlanta-based iMove, whose name stands for "independent movement."

"I've always been an advocate for what's right, and I've been affiliated with both parties," Mowdy said. "What prompted me to become an independent were the struggle of both parties to gain more power and the lack of involvement or real concern candidates had for people and communities."

The mission of iMove is to create a strategy for neighborhood, community, and faith leaders—and independent voters—to fully participate in the public policy process, help generate new ideas for solving long-standing problems, and overhaul a social service system that has failed to provide empowering opportunities for the poor and the homeless.

Not surprisingly, poverty and homelessness, along with unemployment and the lack of jobs that pay a living wage, top Mowdy's list of the political issues that are of primary importance to her as an independent.

"I believe that the society that we live in is far too opulent for homelessness to be an issue in the twenty-first century," she says. "I don't think we'll make much of a difference until we gather people [together]; there's strength in numbers. In the prisons system and the homeless structure there is an unprecedented amount of people who do not vote. [We need to] educate them."

Neither Mowdy nor iMove is focused on voting independents into office. "The focus is to create an environment that includes people. iMove is a nonpartisan, inclusive movement about including citizens in the decision-making process," Mowdy says. And that's a process, she says, that for too long has been denied the very people she serves every day.

PROFILE OF AN INDEPENDENT VOTER

Jonathan Merritt, 25, Atlanta, Georgia

JONATHAN MERRITT is a self-described conservative independent who is disgusted with both parties and has an inexplicable affinity for Libertarians. To understand how radical that political perspective is for him, you'd have to know a bit about his background—starting with his heritage. His father is Dr. James Merritt, former president of the Southern Baptist Convention; Jerry Falwell was a family friend. Dr. Merritt's political views were no secret to anyone. "You never had to ask how we voted. Our family voted a straight Republican ticket," says Merritt. "We were invited to political dinners, and some of the most active members of our large church were congressmen."

When he reached voting age, Jonathan Merritt followed suit, voting a straight Republican ticket—and believing that a person couldn't be a Christian *and* a Democrat; the two were mutually exclusive. After his last year of college—he attended Falwell's Liberty University—he was elected GOP precinct chairman for the First Precinct in the state of Georgia. "I resigned shortly after," he says. "I had ventured into the belly of the partisan beast, and I almost didn't return intact. It is an ugly place to exist."

Even though all officeholders face pressure from contributors, independents, he believes, have the advantage of "pressureless voting" from a partisan standpoint. They're free to vote their consciences, which Merritt believes is more trustworthy than a "party's ever-changing disposition."

A writer and the senior editor of PastorsEdge.com, Merritt remembers attending church during his college years and often asking a friend, "What exactly was the sermon about today anyway?" Much of the service had been devoted to endorsing candidates and other political talk, with little or no room for the Word of God. Democrats were mocked from the pulpit. "When a church publicly draws a political line, it can begin to overshadow the real reason the church exists," he says. "My experience was not uncommon. It was actually normative. Over the years, scores of progressive college grads left Liberty University and found themselves disillusioned with the politico-religious culture found in so many places." He is currently completing a master of divinity program at Southeastern Seminary in North Carolina.

Merritt's major political concerns today are the war in Iraq, particularly achieving victory so the government can focus on other foreign policy issues, and consistent environmental regulations. Global warming, he says, is stealing the stage right now, but other environmental concerns need to be discussed as well.

Though his conservative Protestant faith greatly influences his political perspective, he is open to voting for a Catholic or Mormon candidate. He considers a candidate's voting record to be more helpful than a claim of faith that may not be authentic. His '08 presidential pick as of the summer of 2007 was Fred Thompson—though he secretly wished Stephen Colbert would run, months before the Comedy Central personality announced his candidacy. ✦

PROFILE OF AN INDEPENDENT CANDIDATE

Lisa Braun, 42, Wenonah, New Jersey

WENONAH, A HISTORIC town of a little over one square mile just south of Philadelphia, is home to 2,300 people—most of them Republicans. One of its residents is Lisa Braun, a former customer-service professional who was appointed to a seat on the borough council in 1996. When the Republicans who appointed her discovered she was a registered independent, they insisted that she register to vote as a Republican.

To Braun, her registration status was secondary to her desire to work for the betterment of the community. Over the next nine years, she continued to serve as a Republican member of the council, but her discontent with the party's mantra—"Keep the Republican control"—coupled with the feeling that she was living a lie, caused her to grow increasingly uncomfortable with her situation.

In choosing a slate of candidates, the Republicans' motivation "had shifted from who would serve our taxpayers well to who would win the election," says Braun. "My suspicions were confirmed during a mayoral election when the committee chose a candidate that was the 'highest vote-getter ever' in our town. I knew this incumbent to be a hands-off mayor who only ran because no one else would. I chose to leave the party."

In January 2006, Braun notified Wenonah residents of her decision to become an independent, citing her belief that:

- Council members have an obligation to vote objectively on issues.
- All people, regardless of party designation, should feel secure that their observations, suggestions, and vision are met with equal weight.
- The historical practice of voting along party lines is an antiquated, inefficient approach to filling government positions. Voting for people and not parties helps ensure that local affairs will be handled with open communication and by people with open minds.
- Ideas from both parties can be fused to create the best of both worlds.
- The borough is better served without drawing lines in the sand that only weaken its human resources.

Braun's political purpose is simple and clear: She focuses on the people and not on the political parties. "I am not naïve; I know that we will never fully eradicate partisan politics," she says. "I do believe, however, that we, the independents, can change the flavor of politics. My goal is to communicate this to others and hope that one by one, people will join in the cause of 'independent thinking.' We can elect good, strong leaders who use their brains, not their political connections or backers, to [restore] what was once a solid system of government, by the people and for the people."

A return to that solid system requires major political reform, Braun believes, starting with improving ballot access laws so more independents can run and bring a fresh way of thinking to the political process—and maybe even be elected. "Campaign reform is a necessity in this process," she adds. "By disabling the special interests, the corporate powerhouses, the almighty dollar will lose its power of influence. Elected officials, generally speaking, have lost sight of their role as public servants and have become puppets of their contributors."

Today, Braun remains confident in the integrity of her decision to become an independent. A Presbyterian and a stay-at-home mother of three, ages 13, 11, and 7 ("the most fulfilling job of all"), Braun believes God has given her the security to stand for what she believes in—the people he created. ✦

★

Chapter Two

Changing America

★

They try to wear you down.
—Mike Telesca, Waterbury, Connecticut
  independent voter

As a newly outed independent voter, I found myself at a loss as to what my next step should be. I did not know a single other independent, or at least not one who had ever owned up to it, so I couldn't exactly rally the troops and organize an independent voters' march on Washington or anything like that. Which I wouldn't have done in any event, being independent and therefore not much of a joiner or rallyer. So I did what I knew in my heart of hearts was the one thing I *could* do: I started googling. I googled every possible term and combination of terms I could think of that related to independent, centrist, moderate, third-party, and swing voters.

Early on, I hit the jackpot, though I didn't know it at the time. Among the results for each term I googled was a link to an obscure group called the Committee for a Unified Independent Party. I visited their Web site, found out that they gave up even trying to organize an independent party, thought that was pretty amusing, and subscribed to their magazine. In essence, I had also kind of, sort of, maybe, halfway joined a network of independent voters—but from a safe cyberdistance. Shortly afterward, a woman from the committee—henceforth known as CUIP (pronounced "quip," which I also find amusing)—

e-mailed me to invite me to join in an upcoming teleconference. My body literally tensed up as I read the e-mail. *They want me to . . . to . . . do something?? To* participate?? *They've got to be kidding! I'm an independent!*

I declined in a bumbling sort of way, unintentionally tipping her off to the fact that I didn't want to get *involved* or anything. In a subsequent e-mail I could almost hear her chuckling; I'm guessing she gets that kind of reaction often from independent voters like me who just want to be left alone.

That was in November 2006. Within a month, the good people at CUIP somehow got me to register for a physical, on-site independent-voter conference in New York the following January. I lived in Florida. This meant I would be traveling much of the length of the East Coast to attend a conference where I did not know a single soul, run by a group I knew very little about, and in an un-cyber environment, no less. What's more, I'd be rooming with a complete stranger. This, I can assure you, is not my modus operandi. But "I heart New York," so I relented.

At that conference, titled "Independent Politics in a 'What's Next?' World," I got a taste of what independent activists are about at the most basic level: changing America. Big deal, right? So are a lot of highly partisan voters. But the critical difference is this: Instead of advocating a particular ideological stance regarding those things that we'd like to change (the crises in Iraq and Afghanistan, immigration, health care, education, crime, among many others), the participants in the conference focused on issues that normally make the eyes of ordinary folk like me glaze over—the stuff of political reform. Convinced I was the only representative of ordinary folk in the auditorium, I sat up and listened and took notes and paid attention, determined to at least try to become extraordinary like the panelists on the stage. Those people were so fired up about the most banal political subjects that soon enough I, too, was obsessed with just-shoot-me topics like redistricting. I had started the day a mild-mannered, independent-voting journalist of sorts, but by noon I was a full-throated political junkie. It helped that the panelists were witty and self-deprecating and hugely entertaining.[1] Suddenly, I was *involved*.

CUIP's strategy for effecting change is a smart one, no doubt born of futile efforts to get independent thinkers to support any particular social issue (the glaring exception being the war in Iraq, but more on that later). Part of their strategy is to change the political process, giving the U.S. citizenry a more powerful voice in the decisions that are made—and in who makes them. Another, and highly significant, element of their strategy is to get independents and third-party activists to work together to transform a political system in dire need of improvement. The five hundred participants at the conference were not simply five hundred individuals; they represented millions of independents by virtue of their leadership in such regional organizations as PACleanSweep in Pennsylvania, the California-based IndependentVoice.org, iMove in Georgia, and United Independents of Illinois. And CUIP's Web site (www.independentvoting.org), the *Neo-Independent* magazine, e-mail updates, and frequent teleconferences keep indies connected and up to date on independent political activity.

Their strategy is working. In 2007, when New Hampshire's Committee for an Independent Voice was fighting a bill that would have had a negative impact on independent voters, CUIP rallied independents throughout the country to enlist the support of their friends and relatives in New Hampshire. Due in large part to this grassroots effort and the testimony of independent leaders in the state, the bill, which was clearly designed to benefit the two major parties, was defeated by the members of those very parties. CUIP's database of national leaders in the independent movement is now enabling the organization to mobilize political reform efforts across the country as the 2008 presidential campaign heats up.

But just what are the specific political reform issues that CUIP and others are so focused on? Well, I can tell you this: They aren't exactly sexy. These are the kinds of issues you would never want to curl up in bed with unless you were there to fall into a deep and dreamless sleep. The common terms for some of these issues generally inspire a collective yawn throughout the land; think "ballot access" and "redistricting." See what I mean? So let me tell you a couple of stories that may breathe life into these issues.

YOUR CANDIDATE OF CHOICE?

On Election Day 2004, I drove to my local polling place intending to vote for the person I believed would have made the best leader for our country at that time. I knew his name would not be on the ballot, but no matter. I could always write his name in, right?

Wrong.

There was no space for write-ins on the ballot I was given. I questioned the poll-worker, who told me that the ballots were not always uniform from one precinct to another and that the decision had been made to eliminate the write-in line on the ballots in my precinct.[2] Granted, I lived in Florida at the time, which explains a lot. But still. I had never before been denied the right to vote for the person of my choosing. I exacted revenge by voting against the incumbent supervisor of elections, who presumably denied me that right, but that did little to either defuse my anger or inspire me to vote for one of the presidential candidates listed on the ballot. After all, who enters a voting booth with Candidate B in mind—a second choice? I reluctantly voted for another candidate, but I was not happy about it. In fact, I was furious, and today I believe the wiser course would have been to walk away. I had always voted in accordance with my conscience, but in 2004 I couldn't.

Which brings me to one way to effect change in America: getting the people we want to vote for on the ballot. Until I began talking with independent and third-party candidates, I was unaware of the sometimes insurmountable obstacles candidates face in getting their names listed on ballots if they're not backed by either of the two major parties, especially if they're running for statewide or national offices. Sure, I'd read a story or two about Ralph Nader's failed efforts to get on the ballot in all fifty states in 2004. What did not occur to me was that if Nader, given his name-recognition and clout, was unable to get on the ballot in more than a dozen states, lesser-known candidates hardly stood a chance. What also did not occur to me was to question *why* Nader's name was excluded from those ballots.

Enter Richard Winger, your go-to guy for all you'd ever want to know about the problems candidates have in simply getting their names on the ballot. Since 1985, this sixty-four-year-old San Franciscan has published *Ballot Access News,* considered by many to be the best source of information on legislation and regulations that relate to the subject. His interest in the subject, though, predates the newsletter by several decades; as a political science student at the University of California, Berkeley, in the 1960s, he became intrigued by minor political parties that existed outside the mainstream of political thought.

"I was frustrated because in my own state, there were no third parties on the ballot," Winger told me in a 2007 phone interview. "That was irritating. I couldn't understand why, so then

I got interested in the ballot access laws. I never stopped being interested in them."

Winger, who does not have a law degree but spent years studying election-law decisions at the Berkeley law library, was first recognized as an authority on ballot access law in 1973. He has since offered expert testimony in lawsuits and legislative sessions across the country, as well as before a congressional committee. In addition, he consults with independent and third-party presidential candidates on the nuances of ballot access regulations. He has a library of some four thousand election-law decisions spanning a hundred years.

And he's convinced that of all the democracies in the world, the United States has the most severe ballot access laws. The laws vary wildly from state to state, and what Winger calls the "hypertechnical" regulations are often so complex and obscure that the intent is clearly to keep minor-party and independent candidates off the ballots altogether.

States that require major-party candidates to simply pay a filing fee and complete the necessary documentation often require so much more of other candidates that it's nearly impossible to get their names on the ballot. That not only limits our choices as voters; it also helps incumbents go unchallenged in districts where one of the major parties historically has a lock on a legislative seat. The opposing party doesn't even bother trying.

In my interviews with candidates, the obstacle to ballot access that they most frequently mentioned was the petitioning regulations. One of the worst states in this regard is Georgia.[3] The Georgia Voter Choice Coalition—which represents the Libertarian, Green, and Constitution parties, as well as independents and others—maintains a Web site, www.voterschoice.org, to garner support for legislation to change the requirements and

to educate voters about just how restrictive the requirements
are. In a striking graphic on its Web site, one affiliate, the Bibb
County Libertarian Party, compares Georgia's petition requirements with those of other jurisdictions:

- In Georgia, candidates for the U.S. House of Representatives
  must submit signatures equal to 5 percent of the number of
  registered voters. In 2006, that equaled 195,475 signatures.
- Illinois, the state with the second most restrictive petitioning laws, required signatures equaling 2.4 percent.
- The national average among U.S. states—excluding
  Georgia, which throws off the statistic—is .5 percent, or
  half of 1 percent.
- The signature requirement to run for parliament in Ukraine,
  a former Soviet republic, is also half of 1 percent.[4]

That last item may not be a fair comparison, but you can bet it
gets the attention of visitors to the site.

To put this in perspective, bear in mind that it takes roughly
one dollar to obtain each signature on a petition (in expenditure
of time, gas, and so forth). But because there are so many vari-
ables that enable an opponent or an elections official to challenge a signature—or an entire page of signatures—candidates
tell me that to be safe, their goal is to acquire as many as a
third more signatures than the regulations require. In Georgia,
using the figure above, that means an independent or minor
party candidate would need to spend $260,000 just to get the
required number of verifiable signatures. Even the larger and
better-known third parties would have difficulty raising—and
justify spending—that amount of money to meet one requirement, for one candidate, in one race. And then there's the number of volunteers and hours it would take to canvass the state

and collect that many signatures. Their money and their time, the candidates argue, would be better spent getting their message out to the voters.

According to Winger, the Georgia requirement is so severe that no minor party candidate has qualified for a congressional race since 1942.[5] But Georgia is not alone. Other states have equally difficult laws. "North Carolina's law for independent candidates for U.S. House is so difficult, it has never been used, in the entire history of government-printed ballots in that state," Winger wrote in a March 2007 news item on his Web site, www. ballot-access.org. The Coalition for Free and Open Elections, an advocacy organization Winger helped found in 1985, participated in a lawsuit to overturn the law that spring.

But Winger has hope that all this will change, and in the not-so-distant future. The reason? Well, that brings us to another yawner, and one of the least understood components of U.S. election law: the electoral college. Independents—and many partisans—want to see it abolished.[6]

IT'S GRADUATION TIME

I'm no expert on the electoral college. Like most people, I can barely sputter out a brief definition without scratching my head, staring vacantly off into the distance, and wondering, *This can't be right, can it?* So let's turn to people who know a whole lot more about this than I do. Among those people is the good professor Thomas E. Patterson of Harvard University's John F. Kennedy School of Government. Here's his expert and astute perspective on the electoral college: "It is inconceivable . . . that the framers, if acting today, would concoct anything as bizarre as the electoral college as the method of selecting presidents."[7]

So why did they concoct it back then? Here it would do our

hearts and minds good to turn to another authority, *Politics for Dummies*: "We are no longer concerned about why the electoral college was created. The fact is that it's there."[8]

Cool. I've read the rationale behind it elsewhere, and it makes my head hurt. The electoral college seems bizarre to me, and it seems bizarre to Professor Patterson, and it seems bizarre to a whole lot of other people in the United States (and the rest of the world).[9]

I'd like to skip any discussion of said rationale and just move on, but as it turns out, there are people who actually *want* to know what on earth the founding fathers were thinking.

If you really must know, the founding fathers were thinking that the citizenry could not be trusted to elect the president.

To be fair, they had their reasons way back when. They figured some evildoer could just come along and manipulate the public into making him their supreme leader. That reasoning is hard to fathom today, with our split-second, real-time communications, the vast amount of information available on every candidate, and our greatly improved means of voting, flawed though it may be. The founders decided it would be best to give the voting power to the states, not to the people, and so they created the electoral college, which also served the purpose of giving smaller states more of an advantage than they would have had with a popular-vote plan. Which *also* means that the votes of voters in the least populated states actually count more than those of voters in more densely populated states. One person, one vote? Not quite.

I say it's time to move on. Let's matriculate to the National Popular Vote plan, which has been endorsed not only by independents but also by partisan politicians and state legislatures across the land. However, even though 75 percent of Americans favor abolishing the electoral college, the National Popular Vote plan doesn't do away with this bizarre institution. The plan isn't perfect. But it does offer a rational compromise. Here's my version of an executive summary of the situation:

- Most states have a "winner take all" system.[10] The candidate who wins the popular vote in a given state wins the votes of all the state's electors.
- The U.S. Constitution does not mandate or even mention this system. I'm certain of this; I've actually read the Constitution.
- Under NPV, states would enter into a binding compact with each other (think Port Authority of New York–New Jersey or multistate lottery drawings), agreeing that their electors would vote for the candidate who wins the popular vote nationwide.

As some see it, the downside is that, for example, the Republican candidate could win the popular vote in Florida, but if the Democratic candidate wins the popular vote nationwide, all Florida's electoral votes would go to the Democrat. Still, the candidate who gets the most votes from voters in the booths would win, which seems fair to most people. (Of course, if you just took the electoral college out of the equation, we wouldn't be having this discussion, but that's much too simple a solution for Washington.)

The plan was launched in February 2006 by Stanford University professor John Koza, a coinventor of the scratch-off lottery ticket, and California attorney Barry Fadem. They believe their plan would correct a long-standing problem: candidates focusing their efforts on a few battleground states and effectively ignoring the remaining states—or paying condescending lip service to them. The NPV plan would force candidates to campaign in every state, for everyone's vote. (Koza, Fadem, and others have condensed the details of the plan into a 646-page book—I'm not kidding—titled *Every Vote Equal*. A free PDF edition is available at www.nationalpopularvote.com.)

What are the chances this plan will succeed? Pretty good, it seems. Part of the genius of NPV is that it bypasses the normal route others have taken—attempting to abolish the electoral college through a constitutional amendment, attempts that have obviously failed. By placing the decision in the hands of state legislators, the plan also bypasses Congress, which is a smart move if you want to get something accomplished.

IF NPV FAILS, LET'S TRY IRV. OR AV. OR EVEN ROV.

There's so much dissatisfaction with the electoral college that there seems to be no shortage of work-around plans that would not require a certain-to-fail constitutional amendment. Here are three that also appeal to independents, mainly because they could help make elections more competitive and give independent candidates a fighting chance:

- **IRV (Instant Runoff Voting):** Voters rank candidates in order of their preferences. So if there are six candidates on the ballot, you would rank them in the order you prefer, from one to as many as six. The candidate who receives the highest amount of number 1 votes would win. If no one wins by a majority of the votes, candidates are eliminated from the running by a procedure described at—where else?—www.InstantRunoff.com. This eliminates the need for a second runoff election, hence the name Instant Runoff.
- **AV (Approval Voting):** Say you have that same ballot with six candidates' names. You'd vote for as many as you'd like

to vote for by simply placing a check by their names. The candidate with the highest number of check marks wins. The preferred site for further information is, of course, www.approvalvoting.org. In essence, you're giving a thumbs-up or thumbs-down on every candidate, hence the name Approval Voting. This one is not likely to be used in nationwide elections, but it's already being considered by a number of municipalities for local elections.

- **ROV (Rank-Order Voting):** Exactly the same as IRV. Also known as Choice Voting or Preferential Voting. Just so you know.

Advocates of these alternative methods of voting point out other advantages: A lesser-known candidate would not be placed in the role of a spoiler, and every candidate would be forced, in a sense, to reach out to the entire electorate, not just to their presumed base. As Mark Satin writes in *Radical Middle: The Politics We Need Now,* "Under IRV, candidates have a built-in incentive to seek out innovative positions that appeal to everyone's best interests [rather than polarizing ones]—since they're competing for everyone's second-choice vote."[11]

And perhaps best of all, these alternatives would also eliminate the need for primaries.

FUSION: WE'RE NOT TALKING JAZZ HERE

Bring up the topic of "fusion" at your next social gathering, and you're likely to get a mixed reaction ranging from a mind-numbing discourse on nuclear energy to a passionate discussion about jazz. Apart from political junkies, few regular people outside of New York and several other areas of the country recognize the word as a political term. But where it's used, it can be highly effective. Just ask Michael Bloomberg.

In his first bid to become mayor of New York City in 2002, Bloomberg ran as a Republican—and as the candidate for the Independent Party. That practice is known as fusion, and it allows two (or more) parties to run the same candidate for an office. Bloomberg knows he has independents to thank for his victory that year; the number of votes he received on the Independent Party line provided the margin of victory over his opponent.

Fusion offers several advantages to independent voters. First, it enables them to vote for a candidate on an independent or third-party line without implying support for one of the major parties. (Many a New Yorker breathed a sigh of relief when they realized they could vote for Bloomberg on the Independent Party line and *not* on the Republican line.)

A second benefit is that it assures independents that the candidate will address concerns that are important to them. Though many independents like, if not adore, Bloomberg's maverick brand of politics, the Independent Party's decision to run him as their candidate was hardly automatic. He and his team had to prove themselves to the party's leadership first.

Partisans, of course, hate fusion—when it works against them. No candidate supported by a major party would relish going up against the other major party plus a minor party or two. So efforts to ban fusion often appear on ballots in states where the practice is legal, and partisans often wage efforts to defeat pro-fusion initiatives in states where the practice is not allowed.

Some independents, though, do see a downside to fusion, and theirs is a valid point, I think: Fusion reduces the voters' choices. If Bloomberg had not been the Independent Party's candidate, there would have been a different name on that line and another choice for voters.

Anyway, this is a political-reform issue that many, but not all, independents support.

"THROW THE BUMS OUT"

Anyone over the age of, well, zero has probably heard someone utter that phrase; not even the womb can shield delicate ears from those words, which are often spoken in a really, really venomous tone and with an indelicate adjective describing those bums. The bums, of course, are political incumbents of all stripes. If you're a Republican, the bums are Democrats, and vice versa. If you're an independent, the bums are "all of the above."

The political reform that would ensure the ejection of these incumbents is the establishment of term limits. We wisely imposed term limits on the presidency way back in the twentieth century, and most independents—as well as partisans—feel the time is well past when we should impose term limits on Congress and do away with the corruption-inspiring, deadweight-amassing, do-nothing-enabling phenomenon known as the career politician.

In fact, according to the Cato Institute, "So intense is public support for a 'citizen Congress' brought about through term limits—national polls have consistently put the number at 75 to 80 percent—that rather than give up after the Supreme Court's U.S. Term Limits decision,[12] the movement instead intensified its efforts and adopted a new strategy. In November 1996 voters in nine states approved initiatives that instruct their congressional delegation to vote for term limits (defined as three terms in the House and two terms in the Senate) or face having placed next to their names on the ballot the words, 'Disregarded voters' instructions on term limits.'"[13] You've got to love that last part. We need more threats like that, along with the muscle to back them up.

Critics say we don't need term limits; all we have to do is vote the incumbents out. I wish it were that simple, and so do the citizens of, say, Georgia, where incumbents often run unopposed because they "own" the district. No one would dare put their political life on the line by going up against powerful career politicians. And if you think the days of buying votes are long gone, you need to brush up on your understanding of politics in America.

Right now, U.S. senators serve six-year terms, and it's a rare senator that does not run for reelection. Representatives serve two-year terms, which means they begin campaigning for reelection pretty much on the day they take office. Some advocates of term limits recommend imposing a two-term limit on all legislators. Others advocate extending the length of the term, particularly for members of the U.S. House of Representatives, and limiting the incumbent to one term. One group, Citizens for Term Limits, offers a hybrid solution: one six-year term for senators and three two-year terms for representatives.[14]

In any event, the issue of term limits enjoys widespread support, or at least seems to. (If you hear your senators or representatives coming out in favor of term limits, check their ages. Very likely, those people are of an advanced age and know, absolutely *know,* that there's no chance that term limits will be imposed in their lifetimes. If the incumbent is young, you should still be suspicious, knowing how shrewd politicians can be in their use of reverse psychology.)

There once was a Web site called ThrowTheBumsOut.com, touted as "The Independent Journal for Independent Politics," but alas, it is no more. Still, there are others of regional interest, like Russ Diamond's PACleanSweep.com. Diamond, one of the prime movers and shakers in the national independent movement, writes this on the organization's Web site:

[Members of the Pennsylvania General Assembly] have some-how forgotten the reasons for which the people have sent them there and have tarnished the reputation of an institution originally intended to protect liberties and freedoms which are dear to the people. In my eyes, they are much like the money changers in the temple of biblical lore.

There comes a time in every person's life when they simply need to stop and say enough is enough. For this one individual, that time has come. Many citizens across Pennsylvania apparently share this opinion.

The current General Assembly is beyond repair. All hope of reform among its current members has been vanquished. They have collectively soiled the concept of public service and are incapable of restoring themselves to the good graces of the people. The correction of these inequities must be assigned to a separate group of individuals, a group whose collective hands are clean and prepared for the task ahead.

I expect to be persecuted, hounded and brow-beaten by those I seek to defeat. They will surely use every tool at their disposal to discredit this effort, to cast doubt upon my integrity and punish me for my desire to subvert the wishes of political figureheads and their various committees.

But that is quite all right. I am one individual, with no family to consider, and while they may break me financially or in reputation, I take comfort in the knowledge that I stand on the side of everything that is right, decent and proper.

Every citizen must make their own decision as to what actions they take, or refuse to take, for whatever reasons they deem necessary. I urge you to join me on this mission to restore honor, dignity and integrity to the halls of our state Capitol. It is for these reasons that I commit my life, fortune and sacred honor to this effort.[15]

See what I'm talking about? I meant what I wrote in the preface, that I have encountered so many courageous people who have pledged "their lives, their fortunes, and their sacred honor" to bring about desperately needed changes in our stagnant political system.

But enough of the lofty verbiage. Back to the issue of term limits. Some states and municipalities have already enacted term limits on certain offices, but these laws are sometimes fraught with loopholes that allow incumbents to essentially serve for life, in some capacity or other. An excellent source for data on your state's term limits is U.S. Term Limits (www.ustl.org), which also provides information on grassroots efforts supporting term-limit legislation. Its motto, "Citizen Legislators, *Not* Career Politicians," clearly defines its mission.

And by the way, every independent I know would support term limits on independent candidates. We're your basic equal opportunity voters.

IT'S ALL ABOUT THE MONEY

At the turn of this past century, a woman who was born just after the turn of the previous century set out on a very long walk. Known as Granny D, Doris Haddock of New Hampshire, who was then eighty-nine years old, walked across America to draw attention to an issue that gets the electorate good and riled up—the exorbitant, shameful, immoral, unconscionable, reprehensible, unacceptable, indecent—dare I say sinful?—amount of money involved in elections across the land.

Enter the issue of campaign finance reform. But let's call it something more exciting, like, I don't know, "Throw the Bucks Out."

Granny D has since turned her attention to matters like immigration, figuring her 3,200-mile walkathon and her subsequent efforts to throw the bucks out served their purpose. But others continue to shine the spotlight on one of the most glaring disgraces of the American electoral system. Here's what one of those "others" wrote: "There is nothing, absolutely *nothing,* more destructive to our electoral process than our current campaign finance system. Thanks to the ever-increasing costs of saturation advertising, candidates are becoming more consumed with chasing money than chasing votes . . . In essence, the big spenders have become vote brokers, selling *our* votes, and the candidates are making deals with them instead of us."[16]

This is one of those issues that seems to have taken on a life of its own, to the extent that it has become smitten with jargon and acronyms. I consider this a "need to know" issue, and these are the only things I've decided that I need to know about it:

- **McCain-Feingold** is shorthand for the Bipartisan Campaign Reform Act, which passed in 2002, making it illegal for political parties to use soft money and regulating the use of soft money (see below) by other organizations. No one seems particularly crazy about it except, perhaps, John McCain and Russ Feingold.
- **Soft money** is the "wink, wink" stuff given to political action committees (PACs) and nonprofit political groups (527s) rather than to individual candidates, campaigns, or political parties. I figure it's like this: Say I wanted to give a couple grand to the Whig candidate, but that's illegal. So I give the wink-wink stuff to a pro-Whig PAC or 527, which then discreetly uses it to get the candidate elected while I politely look away.
- **Hard money** is a contribution, in an amount limited by federal law, that is given directly to candidates or their campaigns. The phrase also refers to coins, which has nothing

to do with politics unless you happen to have a video of the gold variety changing hands on Capitol Hill.

- **PACs** are political-action committees, your basic special-interest groups. Think tobacco. Smell anything?
- **527s** are tax-exempt organizations that exist only to influence elections. Among the best known and most controversial is the Swift Boat Veterans for Truth, which aired ads during the 2004 presidential election claiming, among other things, that John Kerry misrepresented his military service.
- Campaigns cost way too much money.

That's it. That's all I need to know. That and how to do something about it, which brings up the names of groups like Common Cause, a major supporter of publicly funded campaigns; Democracy 21, founded by Fred Wertheimer, who is considered a top authority on the issue; the League of Women Voters and its resource-rich Web site; Public Citizen, founded decades ago by Ralph Nader; the student-oriented Democracy Matters, launched by NBA player and "jock for justice" Adonal Foyle; and Fair Elections, whose board includes Daniel Ellsberg of Pentagon Papers fame.[17] Many other organizations that advocate campaign finance reform can be found through an Internet search.

Then there's the issue of the inequity in laws regulating campaign finances for independent and third-party candidates. That politicians are paying any attention at all to campaign finance reform is largely thanks to the efforts of Ross Perot, Ralph Nader, and John McCain, who made the issue central to their presidential bids. The way the 2008 major-party contenders are chasing money makes me suspect that the issue will not be central to *their* presidential bids.

CROSSING THE LINES

We haven't come close to reaching the end of the political reforms that are important to independents, but we've nearly reached the end of my tolerance for writing about them and no doubt your tolerance for reading about them. It wasn't all that long ago that the very word *politics* sent me running for the nearest exit, so I think I've done all right in managing to write this far without recoiling or regurgitating or both. We have one more reform to go, however, and to me it is by far the greatest cure for insomnia. But first, a bedtime story.

Once upon a time a man with an unfortunate future fondled his feather pen and with a flourish[18] signed the most important document in the history of these United States—the Declaration of Independence. This hapless Harvard graduate, member of the Continental Congress, and James Madison's vice president, had the great misfortune of becoming the governor of the great Commonwealth of Massachusetts, an office he had sought unsuccessfully on several occasions. Would that he had remained unsuccessful!

The unfortunate man was one Elbridge Gerry, and the more astute among my readers already know where this story is headed. You see, dear Governor Gerry oversaw the enactment of a law that redrew the lines of electoral districts. One such district was so blatantly contrived to favor one party, and was so bizarrely drawn—for its time, which was 1812—that the artist Gilbert Stuart allegedly[19] suggested to a newspaper editor that it resembled a salamander. The editor corrected him, calling it a "Gerrymander." Or so the story goes.

Now, honestly, you have to feel sorry for the Honorable Governor. Instead of being remembered for all his grand and glorious and patriotic service to a fledgling republic, his name will always be associated with a manipulation of congressional districts designed to serve the parties rather than the people.

Despite that unfairness to him, everyone else actually lived happily ever after—that is, everyone in the present and future states of Alaska, Delaware, Wyoming, Montana, North Dakota, South Dakota, and Vermont, whose populations are so low that they get only one congressional representative each. Thus they neatly bypass the whole problem of gerrymandering on a national level.

Here's the rub: Some congressional districts today make Gerry's salamander-like district appear downright sensible.

Gerrymandering is but one element of the larger issue of redistricting. There's just no way I can transform redistricting into a scintillating subject, but others can and have. That's because they live on the Internet, where they can use cool tools and graphics. If you want to get a better sense of some of the worst recent examples of redistricting, search online for congressional district images. You may find a salamander or two, but they're nothing compared to the snakes out there. The snake-shaped districts, I mean.

Better yet, play The Redistricting Game. There really is such a thing. It was developed for you and me, though no matter who you are, I can guarantee that you'll play it before I ever do. The game was developed at USC, and it helps people understand the process lawmakers use to create legislative districts. According to the Web site—www.redistrictinggame.com, naturally—"This system is subject to a wide range of abuses and manipulations that encourage incumbents to draw districts which protect their seats rather than risk an open contest. . . . [The game] allows players to experience the realities of one of the most important (yet least understood) aspects of our political system." The game also provides information about efforts at reforming the system, including a playable version of Fairness and Independence in Redistricting Act of 2007, more commonly known as the Tanner Redistricting Bill, which calls for the establishment of independent (rather than bipartisan) redistricting commissions and a prohibition on more than one redistricting following a census. (Typically—and ideally—redistricting is conducted every ten years following the national census in order to accommodate changes in population.)

Another online tool for us ordinary folk is called Gerryminder. It's a redistricting simulation that was developed to help students at Ramapo College in New Jersey get a better understanding of elections, representation, and gerrymandering. Gerryminder promises a "non-boring, experiential way" to learn about redistricting. I suggest you do a search for it; its URL in the summer of 2007 is the kind that's not likely to outlive the popularity of the product.

Independents find partisan redistricting to be particularly heinous for a number of reasons. One is the not-so-small matter of the two major parties colluding to draw districts that give each of them safe seats. A Democratic incumbent, for instance, will agree to a redrawn district that favors Republicans as long as the Republican incumbent returns the favor. That collusion has led to a system in which the *candidates* choose the *voters*. Not exactly what the founding fathers had in mind—and not exactly the way most Americans think the electoral system works.

This results in noncompetitive districts, and the chance that an independent or third-party candidate could make a decent showing in those districts is generally zero. Many independents favor scrapping the current single-seat districts and winner-take-all system (sound familiar?) and creating "superdistricts" in which several legislators would represent a single district—which would almost certainly increase voter participation, fairer representation with regard to party affiliation and ethnicity, and maybe even pave the way for an occasional independent or third-party victory.

That's it. Now let's move on—*please*—to you, the voting public. Or the nonvoting public, as the case may be.

DEAD LAST

I TALKED WITH Richard Winger just weeks before New York City Mayor Michael Bloomberg switched his party registration from Republican to Independent, fueling speculation that despite his many denials, he would run for president in 2008. To many independents, as well as partisans disappointed with their party's front-runners, a Bloomberg candidacy would make the '08 race a *real* race. When I asked Winger what sort of impact Bloomberg might have on the election, he brought up yet another problem with elections: a candidate's placement on the ballot. Here's what he told me in an interview in May 2007:

> Certain states dump independents to the worst corner of the ballot. We're long overdue for some court decisions [on this]. We've had a few, but there haven't been enough cases filed. We need to win some more court decisions saying that when they put the order of candidates on the ballot, it's got to be fair, it's got to be random. Either they have a random sample drawing or they rotate.
>
> I met somebody once who lived in Minnesota. He told me he was going to vote for Perot [in 1992]. Minnesota has easy ballot access; there were probably ten candidates on the ballot in '92. Then he went and looked at his ballot in the voting booth, and he saw Perot was almost on the bottom. And he said, "He's way on the bottom. He's not going to make any headway"—and he voted for Bush.
>
> That was a real person telling me how his vote was actually influenced by that. Under the Constitution that should be illegal. Somebody's got to be on the bottom, but there should either be a rotation or a random sample.
>
> I would think Bloomberg would be hurt somewhat by that factor. I would hope he would go to town and sue these states.

And all God's independents said, "Amen!"

PROFILE OF AN INDEPENDENT VOTER

Maggy Simony, 87, Cape Canaveral, Florida

AT EIGHTY-SEVEN, Maggy Simony says she is "so old I remember being at a rally for FDR at the old Madison Square Garden in New York City, probably in 1940. I could never imagine *not* voting." Those were the days when her Socialist uncle was a registered Republican, because he claimed he couldn't get a job as a union carpenter otherwise. On Election Day, GOP workers would offer him a ride to the polling place. He'd accept but then vote for the Socialist candidate.

Simony was an "ardent Democrat" until the Vietnam War. She then switched to the Republican Party. Despite her busy family life, she read the daily and Sunday editions of the *New York Times* from cover to cover and became intrigued with news about international trade and treaties. "Of course, nobody but me seemed a bit concerned," she says. "It became one of those things that caught my attention over the years." Today, those and related issues—trade, globalization ("[it's] destroying the glue that holds the country together"), unlimited immigration, and open borders—dominate her independent political activity. Even so, she considers herself to be an "eclectic traditionalist" rather than a conservative.

In the early 1990s, when Simony was living in New Hampshire ("paradise for a political junkie") and nurturing an addiction to C-Span, she discovered political organizations and "kindred spirits" that shared her views—and Ross Perot. In 1991, disillusioned with both major parties, Simony jumped on the Perot bandwagon, supported him in his 1992 presidential bid, helped start the New Hampshire Reform Party, served as its state secretary, and remained active in the party until "[Pat] Buchanan insurgents destroyed the party" in 2000.

A native of Hempstead, Long Island, Simony was hired to be a war crimes trials transcriptionist in Nuremberg after World War II but ended up in Berlin instead. There she began dating the man who would become her husband and the father of her three children. He died of cancer in 1973.

Professionally, Simony once owned a travel agency and self-published a book in 1978 on the process involved in opening an agency. She later published the three-volume *Traveler's Reading Guide: Readymade Reading Lists for the Armchair Traveler* and produced two single-volume editions for *Facts on File* in the late 1980s and early 1990s.

In 2008, she says, her vote will go to a candidate who opposed the

Bush-Kennedy Immigration Bill. "The only Republican I would vote for in the primary is Duncan Hunter or—so help me!— Dennis Kucinich, as I see it now," she says. "Ballot access is part of my focus; the two parties have total control over it, and while they may hate one another, they join together to bar a third party." She also participates in Unity08. Her dream ticket? Lou Dobbs for president and Virginia senator Jim Webb for vice president.

"We need a third party for the disaffected from both major parties and to keep the other two honest," she says. "I can't stand either party at this point. The way it is now, neither major party represents the interests of middle-class America."

PROFILE OF AN INDEPENDENT VOTER

Robert B. Winn, 60, Maricopa, Arizona

AFTER A YEAR of college, Robert B. Winn joined the navy and served in Vietnam. Shortly after leaving the navy in 1970, he read George Washington's assessment of political parties (see page 54), found himself to be in complete agreement with what he said, and has registered as an independent voter ever since.

In 1980 Winn, a welder, moved from Montana to Arizona and discovered that "something was afoot" with regard to independent voters in his new home state, where the *Arizona Republic* had described independents as the "least interested and least informed" portion of the electorate. With voter registration running at less than 50 percent, Winn could not fathom why the newspaper would print such an inaccurate description of independent voters.

So he ran for office as an interested and informed independent and started a voter registration drive with independent deputy registrars. He was then appointed a permanent deputy registrar in Maricopa County—but his time in that position would turn out to be very short.

"In 1988 the Arizona legislature passed a law requiring that deputy registrars in Arizona be recommended by the chairman of a political party," Winn says. "Deputy registrars who were registered independent were sent a letter informing them that their commissions would expire on December 31, 1988, and they would no longer be eligible to hold that position."

After a lawsuit was filed challenging that law, the Arizona legislature eliminated the position of deputy registrar altogether, which nullified that lawsuit. As a result of the new measure, voter registration procedures became lax, and illegal aliens began registering to vote. In 2004 an initiative opposing illegal alien voter registration received enough signatures to pass. The state created new registration forms that required voters to show identification at the polls, since deputy registrars were no longer on hand to check identification when voters registered. The new voter registration form also featured another major change: the elimination of a box marked "No Party Preference." Voters only had the option to fill in an area designated "Specify Party Preference."

"A local political party spokesman, now on the state committee of his party, boasted in a newspaper interview that the reason for the change was to stop a 7 percent increase in independent voters that took place between the years 2000 and 2005,"

Winn said. "Now, he said, people were registering as Democrats and Republicans again."

Winn and others brought the matter, a violation of the Voting Rights Act of 1965, to the attention of the state attorney general. His response? "Discuss it with your state legislator." Their response? On July 5, 2007, the first day the attorney general became eligible for recall, they registered a petition demanding his recall.

"I do not regard myself as a spokesman for independent voters, just an individual voter protecting my right to register to vote," Winn said. "The United States government was organized and established by independent voters, and there were no organized political parties until the election of 1800. If I choose to register to vote outside of the membership of self-created societies which are now claiming sole power to participate in government, then it is up to the parties to prove that they can take away my right to register to vote."

GEORGE WASHINGTON AND POLITICAL PARTIES

IF YOU THINK today's political situation is confusing, imagine what it would be like to have no real comprehension of what a political party is or why there would ever be a need for one. That seems to be the situation George Washington found himself in during his presidency. Get this: "Washington, like many of his contemporaries, did not understand or believe in political parties, and saw them as fractious agencies subversive of domestic tranquility. When political parties began forming during his administration, and in direct response to some of his policies, he failed to comprehend that parties would be the chief device through which the American people would debate and resolve major public issues. It was his fear of what parties would do to the nation that led Washington to draft his Farewell Address."[20]

Yes! Fractious agencies subversive of domestic tranquility! I couldn't have said it better.

I read Washington's Farewell Address again recently, for the first time in something like forty years. As I read, I imagined him addressing Congress, his voice resounding through the legislative chambers. But no. Over the last four decades, I managed to forget that this "address" was more like an open letter. I can't believe I forgot that. Really. Anyway, it was first published in a Philadelphia newspaper and then in other newspapers throughout the country. Here are some excerpts that make me want to shout:

> In contemplating the causes which may disturb our union it occurs as matter of serious concern that any ground should have been furnished for characterizing parties by geographical discriminations—Northern and Southern, Atlantic and Western—whence designing men may endeavor to excite a belief that there is a real difference of local interests and views.
>
> One of the expedients of party to acquire influence within particular districts is to misrepresent the opinions and aims of other districts. You can not shield yourselves too much against the jealousies and heartburnings which spring from these misrepresentations; they tend to render alien to each other those who ought to be bound together by fraternal affection. . . .

In other words, the lies—I mean misrepresentations—by partisans really muck up any chance for camaraderie.

> I have already intimated to you the danger of parties in the State, with particular reference to the founding of them on geographical discriminations. Let me now take a more comprehensive view,

and warn you in the most solemn manner against the baneful effects of the spirit of party generally.

This spirit, unfortunately, is inseparable from our nature, having its root in the strongest passions of the human mind. It exists under different shapes in all governments, more or less stifled, controlled, or repressed; but in those of the popular form it is seen in its greatest rankness and is truly their worst enemy. . . .

It serves always to distract the public councils and enfeeble the public administration. It agitates the community with ill-founded jealousies and false alarms; kindles the animosity of one part against another; foments occasionally riot and insurrection. It opens the door to foreign influence and corruption, which finds a facilitated access to the government itself through the channels of party passion. Thus the policy and the will of one country are subjected to the policy and will of another.

There is an opinion that parties in free countries are useful checks upon the administration of the government, and serve to keep alive the spirit of liberty. This within certain limits is probably true; and in governments of a monarchical cast patriotism may look with indulgence, if not with favor, upon the spirit of party. But in those of the popular character, in governments purely elective, it is a spirit not to be encouraged. From their natural tendency it is certain there will always be enough of that spirit for every salutary purpose; and there being constant danger of excess, the effort ought to be by force of public opinion to mitigate and assuage it. A fire not to be quenched, it demands a uniform vigilance to prevent its bursting into a flame, lest, instead of warming, it should consume.

I think I'm in love. Especially when he writes that the party spirit "serves always to distract the public councils and enfeeble the public administration. It agitates the community with ill-founded jealousies and false alarms; kindles the animosity of one part against another . . . it is a spirit not to be encouraged."

By being an independent, I've chosen not to encourage that spirit. My very first president would be proud, I'm sure.

★

Chapter Three

Changing America, Part 2

★

*People say you're wasting your vote if you don't vote
for a Republican or a Democrat. I believe it's the
opposite. You're wasting your vote if you do.*
—Larry Reinsch, Iowa
    State organizer for independent voters

Remember how I said I valiantly voted for McGovern in my first-ever voting opportunity back in '72? Shoot, I wasn't even from Massachusetts.[1] I just knew Nixon was the crook he later denied being. And I had taken the war in Vietnam personally, as I watched one friend after another return from Southeast Asia forever changed, and not for the better. There were lots of other factors, of course, and I do think I cast my vote as much for McGovern as I cast it against Nixon. That may have been the last time I actually voted *for* a presidential contender, though it was only a partial thumbs-up.

Regardless of how predictably cynical I was about politics at the time—I was a college senior, after all, and I had come of age as a counterculturalist—I never questioned whether or not my vote would be counted. This was the U.S. of A., for cryin' out loud. You vote for a candidate, someone counts your vote and adds it to everyone else's vote for that candidate, and the total reflects the number of actual votes that candidate received, right? Forgive my naïveté.

I *think* my 1972 vote was counted. It never occurred to me

that some unintentional error or intentional manipulation could have nullified that vote. Under the category of Other Things That Never Occurred to Me over the Years are these items:

- By registering with a major party (as I did in '72), my signature on a petition for a candidate not belonging to that party could have been challenged and disqualified. Huh?
- Not everyone in the country used the same ballot I used, or the same type of ballot, or a ballot with the same presidential candidates listed on it.
- Heck, not everyone used the same kind of machine or booth or sign-in procedure.
- And not everyone registered under the same set of laws and regulations.
- Speaking of which, there was no good reason why I had to register thirty days in advance.
- Still, I had it good. Voters in poorer precincts faced insurmountable obstacles caused by election boards—or the candidates themselves.
- What's more, candidates and the party faithful were working overtime in other parts of the country to *discourage* people from voting.
- Those poll taxes that I learned about in history class? The ones that kept blacks (and, as I later learned, Native Americans) from voting? The ones that we thought were long gone? They would make a comeback under a different guise.
- Tuesday is a truly odd day to hold elections.
- The polls close awfully early for a weekday.
- This stuff makes the electoral college look slightly less bizarre. Slightly.

What makes the first few items on the list particularly upsetting to me is that in the summer of 1972 I audited a course on presidential elections. I apparently learned very little. And to think I could have been partying all summer instead.

FORGET THE PARTYING

So what makes voting problems a specifically independent-voter issue? We're all potential victims of voter suppression, whether we're party-affiliated or not. But here's the thing: When accidents or basic ineptitude isn't a factor in those problems, dirty tricks by the major parties *are*. There's proof galore of this.

Consider this quote from Republican strategist Paul Weyrich, one of the founders of the Heritage Foundation and Moral Majority: "I don't want everybody to vote. Elections are not won by a majority of the people. They never have been from the beginning of our country and they are not now. As a matter of fact, our leverage in the elections quite candidly goes up as the voting populace goes down."[2]

That's right, you know. It's to the Republicans' advantage to find ways of discouraging typical Democratic voters from casting a ballot. And you Dems out there, don't kid yourselves. Efforts aimed at voter suppression and manipulation aren't confined to one party.

This is why many of us became independents in the first place. We could not abide being affiliated, aligned, identified, or in any way associated with two parties whose sole purpose for existence has degenerated into acquiring power and keeping that power by any means possible.

I read an article recently about legislative corruption in which the writer opined that we expect better of our rulers. Well, of course we do. But said writer made a connotative blunder by using the word *ruler*.[3] By strict definition, that word can mean a head of state or someone who passes laws and all that. But it can also mean an all-powerful sovereign leader, and doggone it, in a democracy, legislators are supposed to serve the people, not rule over them. Too many of our legislators believe they have the right to lord it over us. They don't.

As a child, I would occasionally hear someone—usually an old white guy, *at least* thirty or so—barking at a postal worker, "I pay your salary!" I'd hide behind my mother as we stood in line for stamps, hoping the old guy wouldn't start yelling at me next. Well, here I am today, an old white woman of *at least* thirty or so, wanting to get in the faces of various members of the three branches of government and bark those same words. Only those words are meaningless, because there isn't a single high-ranking member of government to whom those words would matter. I have a feeling that "salary" is a meaningless concept to millionaire representatives and appointees. So we have to change the words, but the sentiment remains the same. We have the power to vote them out of office, or impeach them, or recall them, if only we would use it.

Oh well. Let's look at some of the factors that affect us as voters—and that need fixing.

DECLARATION OF INDEPENDENTS

This one really rankles me—the terminology some states require nonpartisans to use when we register to vote. For the longest time it incensed me that I couldn't register as an independent. But I lightened up when I realized there are lots of parties out there with the word "independent" as part of their official names; I can see the confusion that could cause. Here's a lineup of ten states (the first four are states where I've lived; the rest are random) and the language nonpartisans must use when registering:

- **Colorado:** "Unaffiliated." Good. Simple, clear, and direct.
- **Delaware** (I thank God for this most reasonable of states, my home for five years free of government intrusion): A multitude of choices, including "non-partisan" and "unaffiliated."
- **Florida:** "No Party Affiliation." No argument here.
- **New Jersey:** "No, I do not wish to declare a political party affiliation at this time." (Meaning what? That *of course* I will want to declare at some future time?)
- **California:** "I Decline to State a Political Party." "Decline to State" is the fastest-growing category in California. That's a good thing, but I can, and will, quibble here. "Decline to state" sounds coy at best and cagey at worst. It reminds me of news stories in which people decline to comment on a question posed to them. Makes me think they're guilty as sin, you know?
- **Oregon:** "Not a member of a party." You almost expect Oregonians to insist on adding ". . . and no intention of ever joining one."
- **North Dakota:** There's no voter registration here and no need for it. I guess everyone knows everyone else and rural poll-workers pass the time on Election Day saying stuff like, "Here comes that Democrat from over by Cannonball River."
- **Iowa:** "No Party." What's weird is that there's no option for registering with a minor party. Your choices are Democrat, Republican, and No Party. Every other state I checked has a minor party option.
- **Alaska:** The state distinguishes between "Nonpartisan (no party affiliation)" and "Undeclared (no party declared)." It also makes a distinction between political parties and

political groups and allows you to register with either. Pretty cool.

- **New York:** "I DO NOT WISH TO ENROLL IN A PARTY." In all caps. Really. This may just be my favorite: "Make no mistake about it, I DO NOT WISH TO ENROLL IN A PARTY."

Attempts have been made in several states to eliminate any party or affiliation designation other than Democrat and Republican, in the hope, I suppose, that out of sheer frustration we'll quit the fight, admit defeat, and swell the major parties' membership rolls by adding our names. I can assure you that Ralph Nader—blessings be upon him!—will be elected president before that ever happens.

Except maybe I'm wrong about that. In 2006 Arizona eliminated the word "independent" from voter registration forms and replaced it with "Specify Party Preference." Independent voter Robert B. Winn made this observation: "A local party spokesman from this area who has since been elevated to the state committee of his party bragged in a newspaper interview that the high rate of increase in independent voters in the state had been remedied by this action. Whereas the previous four years had shown a 7 percent increase in independent voters in the state, he reported that since the change in the voter registration form, new voters were now registering as Democrats and Republicans."[4] Great. Just great.

All I can say to that is that the independents I know wouldn't fall for that ruse, and they are not squeamish about declaring their independent status. They have no inclination toward Declining to State. They're independents, and they'll state that in ALL CAPS.

GOING THE FIRST ROUND

There's an ongoing dispute in most states about whether independents should be allowed to vote in primary elections. Right now, around twenty states (depending on who is counting and how fussy they are about the details) have what are called open primaries, meaning that a voter does not have to be registered with a major party to vote in that party's primary. Some states are more flexible than others, such as Iowa, which allows independent voters to register as, say Democrats, vote in the Democratic primary, and then reregister as independents the following day. Ohio has a quirky restriction that requires voters to vote in the same primary they previously voted in, though FairVote notes that the regulation is "loosely enforced."[5]

Closed primaries restrict voting to those who have registered with either of the major parties. But here, too, the laws vary from state to state. Kentucky requires voters to declare their party affiliation by December 31 of one year if they want to vote in a primary the following year. Nebraska says independents can vote in a primary if they register with a party, but they can only vote in a congressional primary, not a presidential primary. The West Virginia voter registration form contains this cryptic note: "You may vote a party primary ballot only if you are registered with that party. However, some parties may allow voters who are not affiliated with their party to vote their ballot upon request."

Advocates of closed presidential primaries consider these first-round elections to be a members-only privilege. "The purpose of a primary is for party members to come together and decide who should represent them," Jon Fleischman, a state GOP official in California, the epicenter of debate on the topic, told the *San Francisco Chronicle* in March of 2007. "If you don't want to be involved as a party member, why should you vote?"[6] There's also concern that Democrats might try to manipulate things by voting in the GOP primary, and vice versa. It's been known to happen in several states, but on such a small scale that it did not impact the outcome of the primary.

Critics of closed primaries argue that they disenfranchise independent voters. In California, the Democratic Party thumbed its blue nose at the GOP and opened its primary arms to independents—not because they cared about enfranchisement, but because they care about independents' support. Currying favor with California's three million "decline to state" voters is probably not such a bad idea.

Me, I don't much care. I'm thinking I'm not likely to get all that excited about a major-party candidate these days, so they can have their members-only party as far as I'm concerned. But many of my fellow independents do care, and they care a lot, so I'll probe a little deeper.

So here are a few more factors to consider. One is that primaries are funded by taxpayers, not the parties. Independents—and partisan types who are open to open primaries—believe that's simply unfair; if you pay for it, you should be allowed to make use of it.

Another argument in favor of open primaries is that they may, just may, increase voter participation. Voter turnout for primary elections in most states is atrocious. By welcoming independents into the voting booths, the two parties could help engage more of the electorate in the primary process.

Finally, there's the element of concession. Given that in recent memory the only candidates with a viable chance of becoming president represented the two major parties, some independents figure they should have a say in who those candidates will be, even if they might not be able to bring themselves to actually vote for either candidate on Election Day.

YOU WANT MY *WHAT?*

My first encounter with voter identification challenges occurred fairly early in my electoral life. A college friend with epilepsy was unable to drive, and that created all manner of havoc in her life whenever she needed to produce identification. I don't recall now what work-around she devised. What I do know is that efforts at requiring identification upon registering to vote or when arriving at the polling place are increasing, and those regulations threaten to become more and more restrictive.

At this writing, the furor over Albert Gonzales and the firing of all those U.S. attorneys is focused on allegations of voter fraud and counter-allegations of fraudulent voter-fraud allegations. Whatever the truth is in that situation, this one thing appears to be a fact: No election official anywhere in the country, of any partisan stripe or hue, has produced a shred of evidence that there's any widespread voter fraud anywhere, on any level. There's plenty of election fraud, mind you, but that's not caused by the voters.

You really would think that at a time when voter turnout is so low, election boards would ease up a bit on their restrictions to encourage people to get out and vote. But as Weyrich so eloquently pointed out, a high turnout can be counterproductive.

Here's what some states and jurisdictions have done to make it harder for people to cast a ballot:

- The number one requirement is a photo ID, which sounds reasonable to most of us. But most of us *have* photo IDs because we drive or work for a company that requires it. We have little comprehension of the time and money it takes to acquire the kind of ID some states now insist on. The poor, the elderly, and the disabled are especially hard-hit.
- After the 2006 midterms, voters in a half-dozen states reported that they were asked to show photo IDs at their

polling places even though there was no legal requirement that they do so.

- In New York City, poll-workers routinely asked minorities for photo IDs—which was not required—while white voters did not need to show identification at all.
- Some states are attempting to require proof of citizenship. That seems like a no-brainer, but it can prove to be a severe impediment for people—often the very poor—who have no birth certificate and no means of obtaining one.

A number of advocacy groups have joined forces to fight both the restrictive laws and the illegal practices. Among them is NYU's Brennan Center for Justice, which has this to say: "Efforts to impose unnecessarily burdensome ID or proof of citizenship requirements on voters could disenfranchise many eligible voters, artificially depress turnout, and lead to administrative difficulties at the polls. As many as 10 to 12 percent of eligible voters nationwide do not have government-issued photo IDs; the percentage is even higher for the elderly, people of color, people with disabilities, low income voters, and students. Many of those citizens face enormous difficulties in obtaining such ID."[7]

The Brennan Center regularly conducts studies of voting-related issues, and some of their findings reveal the problems that more restrictive laws could pose for some Americans. Nationwide, 18 percent of elderly Americans don't have photo ID; that number shoots up to 36 percent in Georgia. About 25 percent of African-Americans have no driver's license or other government-issued photo ID. And 15 percent of Americans who earn under $35,000 have no photo ID.

I understand all the arguments for requiring identification—I really do. I can hear some of them in my head right now. But the insistence on these requirements certainly does point to a pattern of voter suppression rather than voter fraud. I mean, come on. I think if someone wants to overthrow the government and undermine our democracy they're probably not going to do it by voting. However, if "certain elements" of our government have figured out that encouraging minorities, the poor, and the elderly to vote would give the opposition party an advantage, they're probably going to engage in some pretty underhanded efforts to suppress the vote.

Besides, there are better means of ensuring election integrity than those that impose hardships on some segments of the electorate. Practices such as comparing signatures from voter registration forms with polling-place sign-in sheets and providing provisional ballots to those voters whose documentation cannot be verified on Election Day are just two means that would eliminate obstacles to voting.

We should be working on far more important electoral problems. When you clear away all the smoke and shatter all the mirrors, this sure looks like one of those diversionary tactics designed to disguise what's really going on. Barbara Burt of Common Cause and Jonah Goldman of the National Campaign for Fair Elections seem to agree: "Why, when too many voters must contend with electronic voting machines that routinely lose thousands of votes, [are] forced to wait in lines that last for hours, are mistakenly purged from voter lists by the thousands, receive incorrect directions from overstressed poll-workers and face a myriad of other problems, would lawmakers focus on a problem that barely exists? Could there be an ulterior motive for calling for harsh voter identification requirements?"[8]

YOU WANT IT *WHEN?*
In the fall of 1995, I had this unexplained urge to vote. It was an off year; no big contests were on the ballot; and I wasn't the most

consistent voter at the time anyway. I couldn't explain it then, and I don't understand it now. What I do know is that we had moved that year, and I needed to reregister. But it was a season filled with business trips and other demands, and when I went to register, I was a day late. The deadline was twenty-nine days before the election, not twenty days as it had been where I lived previously. Who knew?

A lot of us don't know—84 percent of us, in fact.[9] And there's a good reason for that. Once again, states have different deadlines, ranging from thirty days prior to an election right up to Election Day itself, God's preferred voter registration deadline.

The U.S. Election Assistance Commission, whose mission it is to "Make Every Vote Count," saved me hours of research time and offered several minutes of amusement by posting a chart showing the voter registration deadlines for all of the United States and the District of Columbia.[10] (The EAC is under considerable scrutiny, having been labeled dysfunctional and all, but I decided to trust them in this one situation.) It was a tough call, and there were quite a few runners-up, but I managed to select a few of the more entertaining entries to share with you here:

- **Colorado:** Twenty-nine days before the election. If the application is received in the mails *[sic]* without a postmark, it must be received within 5 days of the close of registration. *To which I ask: If it's received in the "mails" without a postmark, shouldn't the postal service be fired? And this is my new home state!*
- **Georgia:** The fifth Monday before any general primary, general election, or presidential preference primary, or regularly scheduled special election pursuant to the Georgia Election Code. In the event that a special election is scheduled on a date other than those dates prescribed by

the Georgia Election Code, registration would close on the 5th day after the call. *Oh, okay, I get it. Just move to another state already.*

- **Iowa:** Must be delivered by 5 p.m. 10 days before the election, if it is a state primary or general election; 11 days before all others. *Does one day really make that much difference?*

- **Nevada:** 9:00 p.m. on the fifth Saturday before any primary or general election. 9:00 p.m. on the third Saturday before any recall or special election. However, if a recall or special election is held on the same day as a primary or general election, the registration closes at 9:00 p.m. on the fifth Saturday before the day for the elections. *This is a joke, right?*

In another day and age, it no doubt made sense to close registration several weeks in advance of an election so lists could be compiled and any questionable entries double-checked. But I can't see any excuse for the dizzying and complicated deadlines above, as well as others I didn't include. And today, there's simply no reason why registration should be closed so far in advance. If the bean counters inside my computer can verify within seconds that I have enough money in my checking account to cover my Amazon purchase, then my local election board ought to be able to figure out in far less than thirty days that I'm eligible to vote. Or twenty-nine days, now that I live in Colorado. Unless, of course, I use the unpostmarked mails.

How is this an independent-voter issue? Again I sound the drumbeat: Anything that makes it harder for people to vote is an issue that politically active independents are likely to adopt, because we're really good at sniffing out the partisan rats hiding behind those barriers.

I'm quickly becoming an advocate of same-day voter registration (SDVR), also known as EDR—Election Day registration. My independent voter friends in Texas are way ahead of me, with stats and all kinds of impressive information about the benefits of SDVR/EDR. They tell me that voter turnout in states with SDVR has increased 5 to 25 percent. The voter turnout in Texas, which has a thirty-day deadline, is lower than the national average (and in the single digits among youth); Independent Texans are trying to get the law changed in an effort to increase voter turnout.

If they succeed, they'll join voters in Idaho, Maine, Minnesota, New Hampshire, Wisconsin, and Wyoming, who already enjoy same-day registration, and in North Dakota, who don't bother registering at all. In the 2000 election, these states boasted a 15 percent higher voter turnout than states without same-day registration, with Minnesota leading the pack, and the nation, with a 69 percent turnout.[11] The 2004 turnout was even better, at 76.8 percent (or 79 percent, depending on the source). Consider this:

> In 1998, Minnesota's same-day registration—which is opposed by many voter-integrity proponents—allowed 250,000 new voters to mobilize around and elect as governor political newcomer Jesse Ventura, who won by under 57,000 votes. Supporters of a variety of candidates who challenge the establishment—such as Democrats Howard Dean and Al Sharpton, as well as Republicans Gary Bauer and Pat Robertson—face disadvantages when they confront heightened hurdles. Voter-integrity regulations are framed as necessary to protect the votes of regular Americans, but they actually exclude many Americans from the political process and entrench incumbents.[12]

The two major parties have already done a fine job of excluding Americans from the political process. As CUIP points out,

"Voter turnout in the U.S. is among the lowest in the world . . . The national average of 36 percent voter turnout ranks the United States at the bottom of all Western democracies."[13] And 38 percent of respondents to a recent survey on voter registration cited "disgust with politics" as their main reason for not registering to vote.[14] I can't blame them. That was my reason for not voting for a good many years.

IF IT'S BROKE, FIX IT

If there ever was a time when it was utterly embarrassing to admit you were from Florida, it was in November of 2000. I shouldered a double burden; I was one of those rare Floridians who not only lived in the state but also was actually born there. My parents wisely spirited me out of Florida when I was but a month old, and I spent the next forty-four years of my life in exile, returning in 1994 to accept a job offer. Silly rabbit.

Those of us who had remained blissfully ignorant of Election Day snafus got smacked in the face on the morning of November 9, 2000, awakening to a tangled mass of confusion that would never be unsnarled. It turned out to be an election in which we all lost; what we lost was our naïve confidence in the voting process itself.

That year my voting precinct in Florida used the tried-and-true paper ballot method of voting. You filled in circles with a trusty No. 2 and took your ballot, concealed in a paper folder, to a machine that ate it and presumably scanned your vote. No problem.

I won't go into all the voting problems elsewhere in Florida and the rest of the country that year. Let me just say this: The system was clearly ailing, and that year the sickness reached epidemic proportions. But you know what they say: Sometimes the cure is worse than the disease.

Enter a new generation of electronic voting machines.

Here are some tidbits from the 2004 presidential election, culled from a variety of governmental and voting-integrity Web sites:

- Machines in North Carolina erased more than 4,000 ballots and failed to count several thousand others.
- A machine in Ohio arbitrarily gave Bush an additional 4,000 votes.

And these, from 2006:

- In a Texas county where 50,000 people voted, around 150,000 votes were counted; the machines counted each vote three times.
- In Sarasota, Florida, 18,000 votes up and vanished.
- In Arkansas, the tally for one mayoral candidate would have been depressing—the machine indicated that he received no votes—had it not been for the fact that he knew darn well that at the very least, he and his wife had cast their ballots for him.

Voting machines have been known to break down. They sometimes fail to start. Techies who know about the Diebold machines in particular have shown how they can register a single vote twice.

At the heart of the problem is not so much the flawed machines as it is the lack of observable, verifiable accountability during the actual voting process. Poll-workers, and any member of the public who wishes to spend Election Day this way, can monitor certain aspects of voting procedures, but they sure as heck can't see what's going on inside a computer. And if someone has a problem with a malfunctioning machine, what are the chances a poll-worker can solve it?

The thing is, I love technology—when it works. I'm sure that if I had been awake and alert when electronic, touch-screen voting was first introduced, I would have thought it was a great idea, a technological advancement whose time had come. I still think it's a great idea. But now I'm thinking it needs to stay an idea and not become a reality. If my ultrasophisticated pop-up stopper still fails to stop pop-ups, and my ultrasensitive e-mail filter still fails to filter out enhancement come-ons, I'd say the chances that someone could hack into a voting machine to change the results or release a virus that could affect the outcome are pretty good.

Some machines can produce a paper ballot that the voter can view and verify but not access; the machines "audit" the results to look for discrepancies between the electronic ballot and the paper backup. By the time you read this, it may be the law of the land that all electronic machines provide some kind of auditable paper trail. That sounds good, except that the machines only audit 3 to 10 percent of the results, and on some machines, the paper ballot is barely readable. And, of course, printers fail, as hundreds did in North Carolina in 2006.

There are so many problematic factors involved in electronic voting—public access to the software and source code being just one of them—that it's difficult to understand why it has such strong support, especially when the paper ballot optical scanners, like the ones used where I voted in 2000, seem problem-free by comparison.

YOU CAN'T SIGN *THAT*

This issue is one that occupies a slot in my mental file of "Things I'll Probably Never Do, but Heaven Help the Person Who Takes

Away My Right to Do Them." Like hanging my laundry on a clothesline in a subdivision that suddenly adopts a "no clothes-line" rule. I'm not crazy about hauling heavy baskets of wet laundry outside, but I'm insisting on that option in the dry climate where I now live.

It's the same with petitions. I can't remember the last time I signed one—in the '70s, maybe. And I don't intend on signing any in the near future. Most Internet petitions are worthless, as we all should know by now. And often when I'm asked to sign a paper petition, someone shoves a clipboard in front of me and barely explains what the petition is all about. So I gently shove it back. But still. If I want to sign the thing, I ought to be allowed to sign the thing.

But in several states, if I had taken leave of my senses and voted in a partisan primary, I would not be allowed to later sign a petition for an independent or third-party candidate. Excuse me? Is that right? Oh, the minutiae that the major parties waste their time and energy on!

THE RETURN OF THE POLL TAX

What I remember most about poll taxes from my various U.S. history courses is that they are bad, very bad. In the late nine-teenth century, some southern states, still fighting the War of Northern Aggression on their own terms, decided to pass laws that required people to pay to vote. Except that the laws often exempted anyone whose father or grandfather (remem-ber, women couldn't vote yet) had voted in a previous election. Oddly, the "previous election" always referred to a year prior to 1870, when the 15th Amendment, which gave blacks the right to vote, was ratified. (Technically, it says the right to vote cannot be denied on the basis of "race, color, or condition of servitude" so as to include former slaves.) Few blacks, already having been discriminated against with regard to employment, could afford the tax. Poor whites who came to the United States after the specified year were also disenfranchised. And let's not forget the Native Americans who lived in the South.

In 1964, imposing such a tax in federal elections was finally outlawed; two years later, poll taxes were outlawed in state and local elections as well.

So how can any jurisdiction get by with imposing a poll tax today? By devising laws that force people to shell out money for the privilege of voting. They're just not called poll taxes anymore.

The worst offender here is so easy to determine that it's laughable. That would be the great state of Georgia.

In 2005, the Georgia legislature passed a law requiring non-drivers to purchase a government-issued photo ID in order to vote. Here's the catch: The IDs cost as much as $35, and they're available only at the state's DMV offices. Much of Georgia is rural farmland, and many of those offices aren't exactly nearby. But who was expected to get to those offices? People who don't drive: the poor, the disabled, and the elderly. And then they would have to fork over $35 for the privilege of voting, a privilege no one else has to pay for.

Honestly, sometimes legislators are so out of touch with the reality so many people live in that it's no wonder they don't do a very good job of representing us. I'm not poor, disabled, or elderly—not yet, anyway, on all three counts—but I've lived out in the country, and even I couldn't get into town a lot of the time. The action taken by these Georgia lawmakers reminds me of a conversation I had eons ago with the director of a writers' conference. We were contemplating what we should charge for the one-day event. "Well, I mean, everyone can afford $50 for a writers' conference!" he said, completely oblivious to the economic realities of everyday life for so many people.

But back to Georgia. A federal court ruled that the law was unconstitutional, bless their judicial hearts. Other states have tried their best to enact similar laws, but their efforts have been challenged by those who contend that they violate the Civil Rights Act.

LET'S MAKE IT EVEN HARDER TO VOTE

As embarrassing as it was to admit I was from Florida back in 2000 (and beyond), I could still take pity on Ohioans. Their plight in recent elections practically mirrored that of Floridians. And just as then-Florida secretary of state Katherine Harris was blamed (or to blame, depending on who's talking) for the many screw-ups, Ohio's secretary of state at the time, Ken Blackwell, bore the brunt of responsibility for that state's electoral missteps in 2004—like briefly requiring that voter-registration forms be printed on 80-pound stock (give me a break!), after many would-be voters had turned in forms from a newspaper or printed off the Internet on copy paper (usually around 20-pound weight); beefing up the number of voting machines in white suburban neighborhoods by shifting them from inner-city areas, leaving poor and elderly urban voters to face lines of up to nine hours; and refusing to allow inner-city voters to use paper punch-card ballots instead of waiting in line for electronic machines, even though provisional and absentee voters were allowed to use the ballots and polling places were equipped with machines to read the ballots and record the votes.

There's more, but I'm going to take the high road and stick to the Election Day problems. Let's just say that it's not surprising that Blackwell, a former Democrat and independent, lost his bid for governor (as a Republican) in 2006.

You'd think there were no voting problems prior to 2000, given the plethora of glitches, malfunctions, and election irregularities that have plagued some jurisdictions since then. While Florida has shown that these are often equal-opportunity problems, affecting wealthy whites in Boca Raton and other cities, all too often the problems surface in impoverished neighborhoods. Honestly, there are times when even the most logical and reasonable and sensible among us have to admit that those wacko conspiracy theorists are on to something.

One of those times would be any Election Day in the new millennium (I'm counting the year 2000 in that era, millennial purists' objections aside). I could list dozens, if not hundreds, of verifiable instances of serious nationwide voting problems—some that just *couldn't* be accidental—that seem designed to discourage students,[15] the poor, the elderly, and the disabled from voting. I won't, because I've begged your indulgence enough. But the abuses run the gamut of hours-long waiting lines; polling places that don't open when they're supposed to; poorly trained poll-workers; insufficiently staffed and equipped polling places; harassment of minorities; confusing, illegal, and inconsistent application of voting rights laws that apply to ex-felons;[16] purged databases of registered voters; deception; and intimidation by partisan poll-workers. In addition, there are many more electoral issues of importance to independents, like nonpartisan municipal elections; the use of initiative, referendum, and recall, three powerful tools available to the citizenry; and open and inclusive debates. You can find great information on these and other issues on Web sites such as www.independentvoting.org; www.independentvoters.org; and www.indytexans.org.

Let me beg your indulgence one more time: We need to either declare Election Day a national holiday so more people have the opportunity to vote, or insist that polling places open earlier (and on time) and stay open later, though the second option doesn't help people who work two jobs.

That's it from me. I'll let someone far more courageous than I have the last word on voting rights. That person is a truly amazing Texas legislator who, in the spring of 2007, traveled from Houston to the state capital of Austin against his doctor's advice to vote against a restrictive voter identification bill—even as his body was showing signs of rejecting his newly transplanted liver. I'll leave you with this thought from Texas state Senator Mario Gallegos: "When more people vote on *American Idol* than vote for president, we should make it easier to vote, not harder."[17]

PROFILE OF AN INDEPENDENT VOTER

Kat Schrode, 23, Boston, Massachusetts

WHEN KAT SCHRODE first registered to vote in Ohio five years ago, she felt that neither of the major parties fit her thinking, so she registered "undeclared." In 2004 she decided she wanted to vote in a presidential primary but had to declare a party to do so. She opted to vote in the Democratic primary; at the time, she didn't realize that changed her voter registration to Democrat and hasn't changed it back, though she considers herself to be an independent.

"The major parties ignore issues that concern Americans, and so an important role of independents is to force candidates and incumbents to address topics they'd prefer to avoid or simply hadn't considered," Schrode says. "Even major-party candidates have concerns and issues they are unwilling to talk about because it could slide them ajar of their party niche. Shattering the current partisan system would allow for more freedom in the raising of issues."

Schrode grew up in Madeira, a suburban, white, middle-class town north of Cincinnati, and first became acquainted with other independents when she began attending Boston University, from which she graduated with degrees in math and biology. Her newfound independent friends introduced her to COIV, the Coali-

tion of Independent Voters in Massachusetts, as well as CUIP. As she became more knowledgeable about what it means to be independent, she also became more active, by supporting and promoting an effort to legalize political fusion in Massachusetts elections (which was defeated by voters in 2006) and by polling independents on a weekly basis about their thoughts regarding the 2008 presidential election.

"I'm not terribly impressed with any of the candidates thus far. I do kind of like Kucinich; maybe it's an Ohio thing," she said. "I'm not optimistic enough to see an independent having a realistic chance. There's a large proportion of voters who are independent, maybe enough to get candidates talking about their issues, or at least acknowledging that independents exist and might just have an influence on the results of the election."

A research technician in the Alcohol and Drug Abuse Research Center at McLean Hospital, a psychiatric facility affiliated with Harvard Medical School, Schrode also volunteers with the Boston All-Stars, an antiviolence program that produces talent shows in inner-city Boston and other cities around the nation. At the time we spoke, Schrode was planning to relocate along with her job to Richmond, Virginia, and eventually return to graduate school with the goal of establishing her own lab someday. Though she does not consider herself to be religious—and prefers to keep religion out of politics—Schrode does believe religion helps shape a person and thereby influences his or her political views.

Not surprisingly, Schrode consid-ers health care to be a major political issue. A primary political reform issue for her is breaking the two-party sys-tem, a system she sees as an obstacle to addressing other critical short- and long-term issues. "Independents can and should be raising such ignored issues, but until independents are rec-ognized, I'm not optimistic about our concerns being heard," she says.

PROFILE OF AN INDEPENDENT VOTER

Suzi Wanga, 28, Suburban Chicago, Illinois

BORN AND REARED in the suburbs of Chicago, Suzi Wanga says every Christian she knew was an evangelical Republican until she left home to attend Bible college in Boston. There she met Christians from other denominations and some who were Democrats. By the time she graduated from college in 2000, she had realized a person could be "true Christian" and not belong to the Republican Party.

"I could not believe how ill-informed I was about issues of faith, politics, liberal/conservative agendas, the two-party majority and its impact on social justice, poverty, and so on," Wanga says. "I started waking up to the realization that politics should not be a compartmentalized component of my life, just like my faith should not be either."

She started breaking free from the Republican mentality of her upbringing but could not fully embrace the Democratic Party. "I was searching for a place where my faith informed my politics and where I wasn't trying to please anyone but God. I just didn't know how to get there yet," she said.

As a grad student in Los Angeles, Wanga's intercultural studies and anthropology program challenged her to think outside the North American Christian box. The international students she met helped her see the "political two-party circus" in the U.S. from an outside perspective and opened her eyes to international issues. She spent a summer working with youth and adults in the Republic of Ireland and a semester studying theology and culture in Kenya, where one of the oldest living Somali Christians taught a course on peace and justice—even after experiencing brutality in his native country. Her fellow students came from war-torn countries like Liberia, Sierra Leone, the Democratic Republic of Congo, Sudan, and Rwanda. "As a white girl from the Midwest, my perspective on the world was blown wide open," she says. Wanga's husband, Ian, is Kenyan; they have two children, two-year-old Micah and one-year-old Lenorah.

Unsettled by a two-party system that had created an imbalance of power, money, and clout in the U.S., Wanga became convinced that "this duopolistic machine" was harmful not only to a fair, democratic process but also to those who are often forgotten by the rich and the politically powerful. She began to research political parties before the 2004 election and ended up registering as an independent. "To the shock of everyone who asked me which of the two candidates

I voted for in 2004, I said neither. On Election Day, I wrote in the candidate that I believed best reflected my faith, beliefs, values, and convictions. And yet, to my understanding, the candidate is not a Christian," she says.

Some of Wanga's friends and family members scolded her for wasting her vote on someone who couldn't win. "I can't stomach the thought of not voting for what I believe and instead settling for what others around me tell me I should believe. I can't think of a bigger waste of a vote than that."

She says she is approaching the 2008 elections with a deeper appreciation for the political process and a greater conviction about her faith in God. "My faith does not allow me to check off a box anymore without knowing that I voted my conscience and my convictions. My faith informs my belief in equality, social justice, and the special place God has in his heart for the poor. I choose to be independent of the two-party machine and instead search out those who promote, enable, and ignite grassroots campaigns to change culture and transform society.

"Whether or not those individuals are Christians does not matter as much to me, because anyone can call himself a Christian to gain enough votes to win a political office," she maintains. "And we have all seen how playing the Christian card has been abused in political campaigns and political offices. My faith informs my political perspective so that I may be more fully prepared to vote and act in light of the words of Micah 6:8, 'To do justly, to love mercy, and to walk humbly with your God.'"

PROFILE OF AN INDEPENDENT VOTER

Betty Ward, 57, Concord, New Hampshire

BETTY WARD never dreamed she would one day become such a prominent political activist that she would be credited with spearheading an effort to kill a New Hampshire bill that was unfavorable to independent voters. "I don't like being in public," say Betty Ward, who nonetheless has testified twice before the state legislature and has been interviewed by the likes of ABC News. "It's not my forte. I shake, I shiver, I almost have a heart attack the night before." But both times she appeared before the legislature, the bills she opposed were defeated or dismissed.

Ward cut her political teeth during the Vietnam era, when her antiwar family lived with the daily possibility that her older brother would be drafted. "I feel he was the unmentioned casualty, because his youth was stolen from him," she says. He avoided Vietnam, but the pressure on him—and all young men of draft age—was significant. And the stress on the family was palpable; the talk around the table had always revolved around religion and politics, and those discussions became more heated during the war.

Ward experienced a political awakening of sorts when, as a graduate student at Hofstra University, she witnessed protesters at a rally for President Nixon being taken by the neck and pulled out of the demonstration. She recalls voting for McGovern and thinking, "Look at this! I'm going to save the world!" Soon enough, marriage, her career as an elementary school teacher, and having children of her own intervened—until the 2004 Howard Dean campaign.

Ward, who once registered with the Democratic Party, has registered as an independent since her late twenties. The actual wording in New Hampshire is undeclared, to which she says, "I'm not undeclared. I'm independent." Regardless of Dean's party affiliation, his antiwar stance worked like a magnet on Ward, who at the time had two children in high school. "I could put myself in the position of my parents with my brother," she says. "I'm just a simple person, and all I know is, [the Iraq war] is wrong. Even after the '06 vote, we're still in the same predicament. How does this happen? I don't see a great light on the horizon."

She worked on the Dean campaign and was understandably discouraged when the campaign collapsed. But then something happened on the local level that got her stirred up—a bill in the state legislature that would have required independents to wait ninety days to reregister as undeclared following a partisan primary in which they voted. With the help of Fran Miller with CUIP, Ward testified against the bill and found herself waist deep in state political waters.

Independents won that round, but the following year a similar bill was introduced. "That one catapulted me, because I took ownership of it," says Ward. "You have to find yourself in this field, because it's so easy to be led and spun and manipulated into other things. You have to be sure about your core. It can be a rush; it's an insidious drug. It can lead to you getting off what you really believe in. It's hard to speak truth to power. But what do they have that I don't? The only thing is power; that's the only thing that separates us."

Ward has since grown accustomed to speaking to power. She held her ground in a meeting with the Obama campaign in which campaign workers tried to recruit her; she made it clear she was there enlisting Obama's support for independents and not offering her support to him. At an event in the spring of 2007, Ward asked Hillary Clinton about the role and voting rights of independent voters; Clinton—who has taken up a fight against independents and third parties in her home state—failed to answer her question. Ward asked the same question of John Edwards several months later; he admitted that independents would determine the outcome of the election but otherwise evaded the question.

Partisan candidates who expect independents to support them won't ever see that support if they won't engage with independents, Ward says. Most of all, she's looking for a candidate who will challenge the party—and the political system as a whole.

★

Chapter Four

Undecided? I Think Not

★

*I am not undecided. I have decided to be
independent.*
—Overheard at a gathering of independents

𝕴 came to public political passion late in life. I have generally
kept, and still do keep, my voting preferences to myself,
a holdover from my days as a full-time journalist. But I
will admit this: I've voted along the entire ideological spectrum.
Because of that, some people would consider me a swing voter.
I don't. Swing voters in the American sense are Republicans and
Democrats at heart and on paper who cross over to the dark side
in any given election by betraying the party that expects their
loyalty and voting for the opposition. That's not me.

I do, however, feel as if I cross over to the dark side in just
about *every* election, but that's because I think most of the candidates are slimy or I'll ruin the good ones by voting them into
office or I'm capitulating to a system that's been corrupted by
career politicians. There's no betrayal there, since no one expects
my loyalty. No one even expects me to show up.

But these Election Days, I do show up, though I feel as if I'm
showing up for battle.

Given that our political system is littered with opportunities
for protest, opposition, and outrage, I like to choose my battles
carefully. So many battles, so little time, you know? The political
reform issues we just looked at are fairly universal in importance

among independents, but then we each add into the mix our own pet issues, like healthcare, immigration, education, and the like. But there is one other issue that makes most of us hot under the collar: the way we're portrayed in the media.

I once conducted a highly unscientific experiment to see how often the words *undecided* and *independent* were linked by the mainstream media—heretofore to be known as MSM to show my solidarity with shorthand-loving bloggers. There's an accurate algebraic formula embedded somewhere in my research, I'm sure, but let's just say that out of X number of stories, Y percent included the term *undecided independents*. In the resulting equation, $Y = a$ lot.

I hereby testify, as I would in any court of law, that independents—the ones I know and know of, the ones who are independent by conscious decision and not by default, the ones who will go, and those who have already gone, to their graves as staunch independents—are not undecided.

Really now, what image comes to your mind when you think of an undecided voter? A nervous, fidgety Edith Bunker who's afraid of making the wrong decision? A neurotic individual who weighs every factor in excruciating detail to such an extent that making a rational decision has become an impossibility? Or maybe a personality-driven voter who thinks Mitt Romney and Hillary Clinton are equally hot in their own way?

Please. Give us a little more credit. We've researched the issues, watched the debates, explored the candidates' Web sites, and decided that not one of them is hot. We stand in a spirit of harmony with Nora Ephron, who said of a previous slate of presidential candidates, "As far as the men who are running for president are concerned, they aren't even people I would date." I may be going out on a limb here, but I'm thinking I could probably dig up a similar quote from a hetero male regarding the woman who is running for president.

In any event, my independent friends don't fit any of those images of an undecided voter. We are not undecided. We are decided, and decidedly so. Here's what we've decided:

- We've decided that we are independent voters.
- We've decided that we cannot be anything other than independent-thinking, which is what drew us to this political persuasion in the first place.
- We've decided that we will vote for the person and not the party.
- We've decided that we will not be swayed by the transparent and often bungling attempts candidates make to court our vote.
- We've decided that we are a political force to be reckoned with.
- We've decided that there are more than two sides to every issue, more than two solutions to every problem, and more than two perspectives that need to be heard.
- We've decided that as far as it is in our power, we will drive the political process and not be driven by it.
- We've decided that we will set the agenda for our political activity and not be seduced into following someone else's.

Joe Garcia of the *Arizona Republic* suggests that the name *independent* "has a Western ring to it, like the stranger who rides into town, not beholden to anyone or anything." Yes! I like that! However, that description does underscore one of the reasons some voters—not anyone *I* know, mind you—choose to label themselves as "independent"; the word conjures up the image of the Marlboro Man, the classic rugged individualist. Let's face it: Neither "Democrat" nor "Republican" has quite the same ring to it. But calling themselves independent because it sounds somewhat rebellious and unconventional doesn't make those people politically astute voters; it makes them political posers.

Garcia, however, is writing about the real deal. He continues, "Independent voters are a mysterious force to be reckoned with. But bewildered campaign strategists trying to reach them must feel like the uncool kid in high school, wondering: 'Where's the party?'"[1] We have no party, of course, and those uncool kids ought to know that by now.

We'd be far less of a mysterious force if politicians would stop talking *at* us and start listening *to* us. The *über*partisans are mostly to blame for this. We independents pride ourselves on not laying blame, so let's change that to say the *über*partisans must bear the burden of responsibility for talking and not listening. They think they can sweet-talk us into the equivalent of a one-night stand with them on Election Day. That's their agenda, and it doesn't occur to them that we might have something to say to *them,* and every day of the year at that. And what we have to say is definitely not sweet talk. That kind of talk loses its steam over the long haul, which is what we're in this for.

Anyway, sharing the burden of responsibility with *über*partisans for misrepresenting us are the media, of which I am an insignificant and marginalized part. Still, I'm family, and I can criticize my own kin. The thing is this: As long as the media continue to use inaccurate terms to describe independent voters, as long as they see us as a homogenous entity, as long as they perpetuate myths and misconceptions about us, there's little chance that even the candidates who desperately need our vote will ever understand us.

MISSING THE STORY

I've talked with any number of independents who believe the media are biased against us. I don't believe that. On the contrary, I believe the media don't think about us long enough to develop a bias. Understanding us takes too much work. It's much easier to accept assumptions about who we are than to dig a little deeper, explore what it is that motivates and unites us, and discover the diversity that peacefully coexists along with our unity. The independent story is truly the untold political story of the moment.

No one knows that better than Jackie Salit, who helped broker an agreement with Michael Bloomberg that gave him the support of the New York Independence Party in both his initial campaign for mayor and in his reelection bid. Bloomberg had registered as a Republican, and he knew he would need a broader base of support to win—especially since he was not a bona fide Republican and Democrats outnumber Republicans five to one in the city. By enlisting the support of the Independence Party, Bloomberg's name could appear on the ballot on both the Republican Party and the Independence Party lines, thanks to New York's political fusion law. That meant independents could cast a vote for him without voting for him as a Republican. In July 2007, I interviewed Salit, who ran Bloomberg's campaign as the Independence Party candidate. She picks up the story on election night 2001:

> When the votes were tallied, Bloomberg had won by 35,000 votes—obviously a very close election, out of 1.5 million votes cast—and 59,091 votes came on the Independence Party line. So the Independence Party and independents in general were Mike's margin of victory. Without us, he doesn't win. That was known on the night of the election. . . . Every-

body knew that's what put him over the top. All the political people knew, all the media in the city knew, and that was a rather significant fact about Bloomberg's initial victory.

There was one article that covered it, two days after the election, in the *Daily News*.

Bloomberg had actively sought the independent vote, and independents had put him in office. There was no question about it, no basis for arguing the fact. And yet the media all but ignored the fact.

The media had four years to catch up with the story of the impact of the independent movement in New York City, but old journalistic habits die hard. In 2005 they once again missed the story behind the story of Bloomberg's reelection. Salit reports what they failed to:

He again sought and received the support of the Independence Party . . . his vote on the Independence Party line went up by 26 percent, and that was the only party line vote to increase; every other party line vote decreased. In addition to that, he polled 47 percent of the black vote, which was an absolutely revolutionary turn of events in New York politics. The idea that half of black voters would opt out of casting a ballot for a Democratic candidate and choose instead to vote for an independent/Republican is earth-shattering. Anyone in mainstream politics, regardless of their persuasion, will tell you that.

Well, again, suffice it to say, there was one article, two days after the election, that profiled the demographics. It in no way traced the importance and the history of the independents' role in peeling that vote away and in presenting to black voters a way to participate in supporting Bloomberg without having to cast a vote for a Republican.

As Salit puts it, the media marginalize independents in their regular coverage of politics and fail to recognize those moments when independents manage to break through and play a pivotal role, as they did in the Bloomberg elections. The MSM by and large ignore the obvious indications that there are "changing political attitudes and that partisan control of the voters is less effective than it used to be," she says.

IMPACT VS. ISSUES

Equally frustrating to independents is the type of attention the media give to third-party candidates. With the possible exception of Ross Perot, on the national level no independent or third-party candidate in recent memory has garnered accurate or significant media coverage of his or her stand on the issues. One reason is obvious: The media's laser-beam focus is directed only at the third-party candidate's impact on the two major-party candidates. Little if any attention is given to the issues that compelled the candidate to take on the daunting and often thankless task of running for office in the first place.

Consider Ralph Nader. I would bet the farm that the average American voter who depends on the MSM for news and information thinks of Nader as the guy who took on the auto industry and who must be some sort of an environmentalist because of his affiliation with the Green Party. Few could articulate even the barest essentials of Nader's platform in 2004, when he ran as an independent. His call for an all-out war on corporate crime and abuse was a given, but his calls for the repeal of the Patriot Act, reform of the penal system, reducing the military budget by 50 percent over ten years, returning the airwaves to the public, and other major reforms fell on deaf media ears, which meant that Americans who depend on the MSM for news had no idea what he stood for.

And whether you agree with his platform or not, Nader addressed issues that the major candidates gave scant attention to, like our support of foreign dictatorships: "Isn't it about time that the U.S. government stop supporting dictatorships and avaricious oligarchies with our tax monies, munitions, and diplomacy?" Nader asked in his 2000 acceptance speech as the Green Party's presidential candidate. "Isn't it time that our government takes a cue from numerous studies and model projects, and advances foreign policies that support the peasants and the workers for a change?" I don't recall hearing that reported by the MSM or advocated by the major candidates.

Back when I was a beat reporter in New Jersey, each municipality I covered was home to at least one political activist who ran for borough council year after year without any hope of being elected. I recall one man in particular who not only ran for public office but also, during the run-up to every election, walked the streets wearing a sandwich board calling for a fairer property tax structure. This was his one issue, the one point he tried to hammer home during every election cycle. An editor who lived in his borough once asked him why he did it, knowing he was considered a nuisance and would only gain a couple dozen votes. The man said the mission of his civic life was to remain a thorn in the side of borough officials until either they addressed the property tax issue in a meaningful way or he breathed his last breath.

Here's what I think: Though people like him are frequently seen as sources of amusement at best or village idiots at worst, they are sometimes just the people we need in our communities to force our elected officials to do the job we expect them to do. Yes, sometimes those people waste not only their own time, which is their business, but also our time, which became my business when as a reporter I sat through many a zoning board meeting listening to residents drone on and on about situations that affected no one in the room—no one in the country, even—but them. *(Those people have a right to be heard, but couldn't they be heard somewhere else? And couldn't they have the wisdom to sense that inevitable moment when the last holdout in the room has given in to sleep?)* But others deserve the attentive ear of politicians who don't want to hear what they have to say.

Nader is of that ilk, as is any independent candidate who even mildly threatens the status quo. Nader in particular is a nuisance to the major parties and especially the major-party candidates. He's seldom been given the opportunity by the MSM to articulate his platform to a wide audience. He's depicted as a spoiler who has the audacity to steal precious votes from the Democrats—when in fact the true spoilers are all too often the major-party candidates themselves.

DO WE SWING . . . ?

Back to independent voters. Most of us do not consider ourselves to be swing voters, and here's why:

> One of the most crucial, but misunderstood, concepts in politics is that of "swing voters." The term is often confused with *undecided voters:* those who, at any given moment of a campaign, have not chosen a candidate. And the two categories do tend to overlap. But more precisely, swing voters are those who belong to some category of the electorate with an unstable attachment to the major political parties. They are literally in motion from election to election, which makes them unusually susceptible to persuasion based on each party's message, candidate characteristics, policy agenda, and political effort.[2]

That's how Mark Gersh described swing voters in *Blueprint* magazine, and that's why so many of us dislike that designation. "Unusually susceptible to political persuasion"? I think not. "Unusually resistant to political persuasion" is more like it.

Swing voters in the classic sense are those under-thirty Democrats (ex-Democrats?) in Minnesota who, in the 2000 presidential race, punished the Democratic Party for its hostile treatment of then-Governor Jesse Ventura, the former pro wrestler and radio talk show host who won as an independent candidate in 1998. In the same article, Gersh, Washington director of the National Committee for an Effective Congress, noted a twenty-nine-point drop among young voters in support for Al Gore in 2000 compared with Bill Clinton in 1996. Defecting to the Republican Party had to hurt those twenty-somethings like nothing else, but what Gersh calls the "Ventura factor"—"a lingering feeling of alienation from the Democratic Party" among young people who liked Ventura—apparently ran deep.[3] Thanks in part to Minnesota's Election-Day registration and its concerted effort to encourage young people to register, Ventura once commented that independents in the state outnumber the combined total of die-hard Republicans and Democrats (which he placed at 15 to 20 percent for each party).[4] The increase in the number of registered independents has made Minnesota a deep purple battleground state, as has its always-high voter turnout rate.

Another reason why many independents dislike being called swing voters is the media's insistence on carrying the label to ridiculous extremes. Remember 1996, the year of the "soccer mom"? Or 2002, the year of the "NASCAR dad"? How about 2004, the year of the "security mom"? To equate independents with those narrow definitions of swing voters is to do the independent movement a tremendous disservice.

Granted, not every depiction of independents as swing voters is that narrow or pejorative. Mark Penn of the *Washington Post* got it right in a March 2006 article in which he pointed out the foolishness of playing to the major parties' base:

> But in fact, while the base is critical, it's not the whole picture. Behind all the rhetoric, the reality is that swing is still king. The two or three or 10 voters who are the quietest in focus groups, who never demonstrate and who belong to no political party, will be the ones who determine the political course of America.
>
> This is less true in Washington, where everyone has to choose sides to survive, but outside the Beltway, trends show that voters are increasingly open and flexible, not rigid. They are looking at candidates' records and visions, not their party affiliation.
>
> The fastest-growing political party in the United States is no party . . . That shows a radical new willingness on the part of Americans to look at individual candidates, not party slates. It is a sign of a thinking electorate, not a partisan one.[5]

A thinking electorate indeed.

. . . OR DO WE SWAY?

In an insightful article first published in the Worcester, Massachusetts, *Telegram & Gazette*, CUIP political director Jackie Salit responded to the inference that independents are swing voters by adding the element of influence to our impact as voters. We aren't swing voters who simply react; independents, she wrote, are "sway voters, a force able to initiate political events and sit at the political table on its own behalf."[6]

Thanks largely to CUIP's efforts aimed at bringing together independent individuals, organizations, and political parties from around the country, the ability of the independent movement to influence far more powerful political forces is starting to be realized. According to Salit, independents kept opposition to the war in Iraq a front-and-center issue in the 2006 midterms, compelling the Democrats to finally speak out against the course the war had taken. That's the kind of influence the independent movement is hoping to capitalize on in the future—the power to drive rather than be driven.

What most Americans, including independents, fail to recognize is that the nation is not divided into two camps with a smattering of independent voices taking up whatever slack there may be in the two-party system. The reality is that independents are the single largest political constituency in the country. We represent well over a third of the electorate, with some polls placing us at 42 percent. For argument's sake, though, let's say the nation is divided into thirds—one-third Democrats, one-third independents, and one-third Republicans. We should have a place at the table, but as Mark Penn pointed out, we're generally the quiet ones who never demonstrate. So maybe we don't call attention to ourselves, but we do call attention to the issues, as Salit rightly noted regarding the Iraq War.

Contributing to the power to sway public policy is the growth of independent leadership across the country. Wayne Griffin, chair of the South Carolina Independence Party; Cathy Stewart, New York County chair of the New York Independence Party; Jim Mangia and Joyce Dattner, co-chairs of IndependentVoice.org in California—these and other leaders are focusing their attention on uniting independents so their—our—potential as a political force can be realized. Salit writes:

> New on-the-ground independent leaders are coming up around the country, building bases of support among

independent and anti-establishment voters. Their goal is to close the enormous gap between the sheer numbers of Americans who are independents and the actual political recognition and power they hold.

These independent leaders hold to wide-ranging positions on social issues, but share a fervent belief in structural political reform. They are less into the "net roots" than they are into the "get roots" — building tangible, personal and developmental networks of independents who can be deployed into a variety of political activities.[7]

The bottom line, as Salit describes it, is that instead of simply being a deciding factor in elections—no small feat in itself—independents are "deciding things for themselves."

PROFILE OF AN INDEPENDENT VOTER

Bob Friedman, 57, Birmingham, Alabama

GROWING UP IN New York City in the 1950s and '60s—and having a great voice—gave Bob Friedman a personal connection with black America that has guided his life ever since. "I was a member of various do-wop groups in New York," says Friedman, who today hosts a political talk show. "I did a lot of singing and some recording, and won amateur night at the Apollo in 1964; I felt free to go to Harlem when I was fourteen." That was at a time when many white *adults* were afraid to go to Harlem, no matter how much they wanted to see the legendary shows at the Apollo Theater.

Freidman's political activity has its roots in the antiwar movement of the 1960s and 1970s. Later he became a welfare rights organizer in Gary, Indiana, and realized in short order that, as he puts it, society was making people poor much more quickly than any group of well-meaning citizens could help them. "I realized that you have to be involved politically," he says. So he began working on local campaigns for third-party candidates in the late 1970s, as well as the Bronx campaign of the New Alliance Party in 1979.

Friedman moved to Chicago and helped build a welfare recipients' union movement, which he says laid the groundwork for Harold Washington's 1983 mayoral campaign. Washington, the first black mayor of Chicago, also served in Congress and was reelected by the largest majority ever—over 99 percent—in the history of the U.S. Congress. "He was enormously popular," says Friedman, who also worked on his 1987 mayoral reelection campaign. "He was an extraordinary candidate, and he was an extraordinary man."

Between Washington's two campaigns, Friedman got a taste of national campaign work when the New Alliance Party ran Dennis L. Serrette, an African-American union activist, for president in 1984. Knowing of his political work in the Chicago area and his ties with the African-American community, Dr. Lenora Fulani asked Freidman to work on the Southern strategy for her 1988 presidential bid. Friedman said yes, moved to Alabama, and never looked back.

"I worked to get her on the ballot and to raise matching funds for her in seven southern states as well as in Illinois, Michigan, and Ohio," says Freidman. "I was basically on the road all the time, getting signatures during the day and knocking on doors at night. It was very exciting."

In Birmingham, Friedman discovered a much more subdued level of activism with regard to welfare rights, especially compared to the aggressive, militant efforts he had witnessed in Chicago. He focused his attention on independent politics and ran campaigns for independent and third-party candidates for city council and county commission.

And then, in 1992, longtime black activist Albert Turner, who worked with Martin Luther King Jr., ran in the Democratic primary for a seat on the Perry County commission and won by 29 votes—until four days later, when someone "discovered" another box of ballots containing exactly 30 votes for his opponent. Friedman was able to get Turner on the ballot in the general election as the county commission candidate for the New Alliance Party. He won by 133 votes.

"The Democrats promptly kicked him out of the party, and went to work making it even more difficult to get on the ballot," Friedman says. "They tripled the ballot access requirements in the state." Previously, a petition candidate needed signatures equaling 1 percent of the vote cast in the previous governor's race; now it was 3 percent.

Friedman worked on the 1994 and 1996 Ross Perot campaigns and over the years continued to run local candidates on the newly formed Patriot Party line, which had attracted a fair number of black voters and candidates. "But this time the Democratic Party was going nuts because they were very concerned about losing the black vote, because there were more African-Americans that were interested in leaving the Democratic Party, particularly because they were the kind of very junior partner in that party," he says. "They weren't being paid attention to very much."

More recently, Friedman and others took the remnants of various third-party campaigns and parties, set up a phone bank, made cold calls out of the phone book, and created the Alabama Independent Movement. He made an unsuccessful bid for city council in 2001.

Today, Friedman serves on the Birmingham housing authority and works as operations manager and sales manager at WJLD-AM. He's also working to put together a coalition of Greens, Libertarians, and independents called Independent Alabama.

PROFILE OF A THIRD-PARTY CANDIDATE

Carl Romanelli, 48, Wilkes-Barre, Pennsylvania

IN 2006, THE Green Party of Pennsylvania selected Carl Romanelli to run for the U.S. Senate against Republican Rick Santorum and Democrat Bob Casey Jr. Romanelli set out to acquire the 67,070 petition signatures he needed to get his name on the ballot. He submitted nearly 95,000. And that's when everything broke loose.

The Democrats alleged that Santorum had contributed to Romanelli's campaign because the Republicans believed a Green candidate would hurt Casey's chances of being elected. Romanelli denies that allegation and says he ran a clean campaign. "What's appalling is that despite the [ballot access] barriers the state put up, we were able to meet them," Romanelli says. "We accomplished something no one has ever done in this Commonwealth before. I'm so sick and tired of everyone trying to give Rick Santorum and the Republicans credit for that." From the outset of his campaign, he made public appeals for help from both Republicans and Democrats; two Republican friends responded.

Before he submitted the petitions, he and his campaign workers sifted through the 99,802 signatures they had acquired and crossed out about 5,000 that appeared to them to be invalid in a random sampling. "No candidate in the history of the state has ever done that before," Romanelli says. "We wanted to file a package that had extreme integrity."

The department of state reviewed the signatures, verified that Romanelli had qualified for the ballot, and gave opponents a week to file a challenge. The Democratic Party publicly denounced his petitions as "wrought with fraud and forgeries," he says. They cited names like Mickey Mouse, Mona Lisa, George Bush, and Robert Redford, but in the challenge they filed with the state, they listed only a total of fifty-one names that appeared fraudulent out of the 95,000 signatures.

What happened next can only be described as a nightmare. The Democrats, according to Romanelli, began challenging tens of thousands of signatures in a blanket manner, without having a specific reason for doing so. The party also managed to circumvent a process that would have had a judge look at the signatures and replaced it with a process requiring nine Democrats and nine Green Party members to work together at the state department building in Harrisburg to verify or exclude the challenged signatures. Finding nine people who could devote four weeks to this process wasn't so hard for the Democrats, with their 3-million-plus membership in Pennsylvania, but it was a requirement that was nearly impossible for the Greens, and their 17,000 statewide membership, to meet. At one point, one Green Party helper was in a car accident, a second had an emergency situation at the business he owned, and a third had to attend a funeral—the funeral of his mother. The Democrats threatened to cite the Greens with contempt.

There's much more to this story, but suffice it to say that the Democrats succeeded in keeping Romanelli off the ballot. A few months after the election, a Commonwealth Court ordered Romanelli to pay more than $80,000 in the Democratic Party's legal fees (the party originally sought $89,668 but "generously" reduced the amount by a little less than 10 percent). According to Romanelli, the legal fees were much higher. Romanelli appealed to the Pennsylvania Supreme Court regarding the ballot-displacement issue, and eventually to the U.S. Supreme Court, which declined to hear the case. In May of 2007, the fines and costs were appealed to the Pennsylvania Supreme Court. As of September 2007, the Court had not made a decision.

Romanelli, a rail-industry consultant, worked as a Democratic political operative for many years. But he also has been cautioning about the demise of the Democratic Party for about twenty-five years and "out of disgust" eventually left the party. "The two things in my life that I thought I would never change are my religion and my political party, because I assumed that both are naturally flawed, we're all born into one, and it's our duty to be rational and reform from within," he says. "Well, being raised thinking my religion was Italian Catholic Democrat, I am now a Green Party Presbyterian."

One outcome of the 2006 election debacle was a documentary. A film and history student from Penn was covering the Senate race, and Romanelli was originally just one of several candidates the filmmaker was following. "As things got absurd, he couldn't believe what he was seeing, and it led to a totally different direction for the movie," Romanelli said. The resulting film was shown at film festivals and screenings around the country. Its title? *It Ain't Easy Being Green*, of course. ✦

PROFILE OF AN INDEPENDENT VOTER

Craig Detweiler, 43, Culver City, California

CRAIG DETWEILER calls himself "the world's oldest living Gen-Xer," having grown up during the Vietnam War. What began in the 1960s, he says, took full root in his life, making him "fiercely independent" and steering him in a creative direction both professionally and academically.

Currently he's the director of Reel Spirituality, a filmmaking institute at the Brehm Center for Worship, Theology, and the Arts at Fuller Theological Seminary in Pasadena, California. Detweiler is also a film professor at Fuller and a screenwriter, with the 1999 Disney Film *The Duke* to his credit, among other movies.

And best of all, in my astute opinion, he's the producer of *Purple State of Mind*, a feature documentary about the red/blue divide in the United States.

"I was raised Republican, and the further I moved in my spiritual journey the more Democratic I became," says Detweiler. "I think Jesus certainly pushed me toward there, to caring about the 'least of these.'"

Too many people of faith, he believes, have essentially sold their vote to special interests rather than kingdom interests, creating what he calls an "unholy marriage" between faith and politics. He says those two arenas of life are related, and if one

party represented everything that Jesus taught, Detweiler would have less of a problem with the relationship between religious and political life. But both parties, he believes, have veered far off that course, and today, overt partisanship in the church leaves him cold—or rather, hot.

"I've been in churches where the political voter guides are available in the lobby, and I'm always dismayed at how single-issue they were; our problems are more complex than that," he says. "I've walked out of many churches seething with anger when what is an occasion to worship God has turned into an occasion to woo voters."

It has also become an occasion to misrepresent much of what Jesus was about. One of Jesus' comments—that people must "render unto Caesar" what belongs to Caesar—is among those that are profoundly misunderstood, Detweiler believes. "It has come to mean 'pay your taxes,'" he says. "In the context of the day it was much more of a challenge to the political authorities. You can see it in the shocked reaction of the people. If he meant 'pay your taxes,' why would people be offended? You're being challenged in that passage to question Caesar and not give your blind allegiance to those principalities and powers. It's more of a question about Caesar; is it possible to cooperate with him? Jesus was skeptical about forming alliances with those interested in playing a different game."

Particularly since the 2003 publication of *A Matrix of Meanings: Finding God in Pop Culture*, which he wrote with Barry Taylor, Detweiler has been considered a significant authority on the intersection of faith and culture—a vibrant field within evangelicalism and progressive faith expressions like the emerging church. Unlike many of their predecessors, evangelicals today—particularly younger ones—and progressive people of faith believe Christians have a responsibility to engage and befriend the wider culture, without judgment, criticism, pressure to convert, or any other agenda. One of the keys to engaging the culture, Detweiler believes, is listening:

"When you see Jesus in the gospel you see him constantly shifting strategies, depending on who he was talking to," Detweiler points out. "He saw through the unholy marriage between faith and politics in his own day and tried to call people to a different kind of allegiance—to join God's party."

★

Chapter Five

The Online Electorate

★

*It is a movement that attracts and engages people
because it empowers them, not because it gives them
yet another flawed "leader" to follow. It returns
power where it belongs in a democracy—to the
people. In this new movement, people control their
own destiny.*
—Jerome Armstrong and Markos Moulitsas
    Authors of *Crashing the Gate: Netroots,
    Grassroots, and the Rise of People-Powered
    Politics*

In a previous lifetime, I was a mail-order fanatic, especially during the five years we lived in an isolated, rural area. The closest town, eight miles on the other side of an assortment of fields and pastures and junkyards, boasted one office-supply store whose owners apparently reckoned that anyone worth selling to could jolly well get to the store between the hours of 9:00 and 5:00 on any day that didn't belong to a weekend. I was among those who couldn't jolly well do that, so I kept UPS hopping with frequent deliveries of office supplies, rare or unusual books, and homeschooling materials (yes, I was one of *those* mothers) that I could not find locally.

And the library—now there was a place where I logged many a frequent-patron hour. One of my constant companions during library outings was the *Directory of Associations*. I'd pull that volume from the reference shelf and pore over it as I searched for organizations related to articles I was writing or groups whose purpose resonated with whatever I was passionate about at the time.

That was *so* 1980s.

Within a few short years, I'd be able to accomplish all of the above without ever getting in my car or picking up the phone or licking a stamp. Today the Internet is my fifth or sixth love, depending on which family members and friends I choose to include in the tally on any given day.

It's hard for my daughters to imagine life without the Internet, but it's even harder for me to imagine it—because I remember it. I remember what it was like to do research for my writing projects in those pre-Web days or track down a company that distributed a desperately needed, hard-to-find part for one of the many outdated machines and appliances we were trying to keep in running condition. I remember that life, and I can't imagine going back to it.

Still, for whatever reason, it didn't occur to me until several years ago that I could find like-minded political types on the Internet, which is probably the greatest single indication of my lack of involvement and interest in politics up to that time. For everything else, the Internet had become my primary means of obtaining information and making contact with individuals and organizations.

But ever since the first time I googled "independent voter," there's been no turning back. And with good reason: Without an organized party—which most of us don't want—independent voters have found the Internet to be a lifeline to help us find each other and stay connected once we do. Had I not searched the Web, I'm convinced I'd still be wandering the independent political wilderness all by myself, feeling ever more freakish with each step.

YOU CAN THANK THE HANKSTER

One of the first sites I discovered in my search for independent voters was a blog called The Hankster (http://grassrootsindependent.blogspot.com). Little did I know that in my initial search I had stumbled upon[1] one of the most valuable Web-based resources for independent voters and candidates. Each day The Hankster keeps us informed about news and legislative actions of interest to independents. Launched in the spring of 2006 by longtime political activist Nancy Hanks, the blog site grew out of research she was already doing for the *Neo-Independent* magazine.

"I have been involved with independent politics since the '70s, long before the advent of Internet communications," Hanks told me. "I would say the Internet has enabled independents to expand and deepen our reach and influence. A lot has been written about the power of the blogs over the last five to six years as a communication vehicle. That said, organizing the unorganized is still a tedious 'bricks and mortar' process that takes lots of stick-to-it-iveness."

What independent activists are dealing with first and foremost, she said, is creating a "market" for independent voters. "There's no ready-made marketplace like there is for Democrats and Republicans, or for ideological strands of thought like liberals and conservatives," Hanks pointed out. "We are creating something quite new; it isn't there yet. We can draw from many sources—disaffected voters, voters who don't feel they fit into the current categories, the 'fed-ups,' etc. It's somewhat like herding cats!"

We cats, though, are slowly shedding our detached feline ways and actually networking with each other. The Internet is a big factor in facilitating that. I mean, when you can meet other independents online, you don't have to physically rub elbows with each other, you know? It's a whole lot easier to remain psychologically independent when you can hang out in cyberspace. Plus, you don't have to provide refreshments. So herding us may be a challenge, but at least we can now be found.

Anyway, Hanks, a New Yorker and a full-time grant-writer for an international homeless youth program, considers her blog site to be a vehicle for creating an activistic, rather than a journalistic, online independent voice, one that avoids the pitfall of becoming an ideological soapbox. Among her joys has been discovering other nonpartisan bloggers who want to help create a "new independent culture." "Within a few weeks of publishing The Hankster, a number of independents—Zeb Pike in Maine, Pete Abel in St. Louis—started their own blogs, inspired by mine," Hanks says. "More recently, A Registered Voter, An Ordinary Person, and Politics in America have joined in the online effort to 'blog independent.'"

Netroots activists—political activists who use blogs, social networking sites, and the like to promote Internet-based grassroots activities—are largely "Democratic Partyists and pretty traditional in their approach: talk about the hot-button issues and complain about the Republicans," Hanks says. "Blogs like MyDD and TPMCafe, or Huffington Post and Daily Kos are huge and well-established. There are some sizable independent blogs which claim centrism as their beat—The Moderate Voice and WatchBlog are two. I think all these efforts to get beyond the mainstream media are good."

Among the most prominent and influential political bloggers are Jerome Armstrong, a Democratic strategist and founder of the MyDD blog, and Markos Moulitsas, who founded the liberal DailyKos blog, which attracts some 600,000 visitors each day. Together they wrote the 2006 book *Crashing the Gate: Netroots, Grassroots, and the Rise of People-Powered Politics*, in which they had this to say about netroots activism: "They may view us in D.C. as barbarians at the gate, but we are not armed with pitchforks and torches. Technology has opened up the previously closed realm of activist politics to riffraff like us. . . . Trying to stop us is a losing proposition."[2]

STRIKING FEAR IN THE HEARTS OF POLITICIANS

If established partisans like Armstrong and Moulitsas consider themselves riffraff, I hate to think of the term grassroots independents should use to describe ourselves. Whatever that descriptor turns out to be, we can express a certain measure of solidarity with other online riffraff in this one sense: Trying to stop us is indeed a losing proposition. And The Establishment is scrambling to come to terms with this unprecedented, Internet-induced turn of events; you can *really* see it in the presidential candidates' Web sites and efforts like the online presidential campaign known as Unity08 (more about that in chapter 9). Despite their foray into online campaigning, you have to believe that the power of the Internet scares the daylights out of career politicians; the last thing they need is an unruly bunch of disgruntled, anti-establishment, nonpartisan types getting together and making life miserable for them.

Among the major political events in recent years credited to the netroots (a term coined by Armstrong, by the way[3]) are these:

- Bloggers propelled Howard Dean to the forefront in the early stages of the 2004 presidential campaign. When Democratic Party leaders sabotaged Dean's campaign, the netroots relentlessly lobbied voting members of the Democratic National Committee to elect Dean as chairman, which they did in 2005.

- When then-Senate Majority Leader Trent Lott, speaking at Strom Thurmond's one hundredth birthday party, made a remark that seemed to support racial segregation, bloggers Joshua Josiah Marshall and Glenn Reynolds kept the story alive long after the MSM had moved on, resulting in the Mississippi Republican's resignation. "Bloggers claim I was their first pelt, and I believe that. I'll never read a blog," Lott told the *Christian Science Monitor*.[4]

- Democrat Jim Webb's victory over incumbent Republican George Allen in the 2006 U.S. Senate race in Virginia is largely credited to bloggers who waged a "Draft Webb" campaign encouraging him to declare his candidacy. Then there's that *other* Internet factor in his election: the videos on YouTube of Allen's infamous "macaca" comment and of Allen staffers taking down a Webb supporter at a campaign event in Charlottesville.[5]

- Not election-related, but following the Hurricane Katrina disaster bloggers Glenn Reynolds (Instapundit) and N.Z. Bear (The Truth Laid Bear) drew attention to pork-barrel spending through an effort known as Porkbusters, which was designed to redirect money from pork-barrel projects to hurricane relief.[6]

The ability to have that kind of effect on political events was unheard of prior to the Internet age. Even so, independent bloggers haven't garnered that kind of clout yet, at least not in any way that's visible to the public. Behind the scenes, though, a grassroots movement of independent bloggers is also circumventing both the MSM and politics-as-usual to disseminate information that partisan career politicians wish we didn't know. Among the blog sites that offer original reporting from a nonpartisan perspective is one that Hanks mentioned,

TheModerateVoice.com, which boasts a staff of experienced journalists of varied professional backgrounds and political persuasions. Like the best of the independent Web and blog sites, The Hankster and the Moderate Voice offer extensive links to other independent and third-party sites.

PEOPLE-POWERED POLITICS

Online activism has given rise to what Armstrong and Moulitsas call "people-powered politics," which may prove to be democracy in its purest form. That sounds so idealistic that even I have a hard time believing it, and I'm the one who wrote it. Power is so susceptible to corruption, and though I'd love to believe that the power of grassroots activism is incorruptible, I really do know better. But pretend with me for a moment that we can harness the power of the Internet for the good of the country and redeem the political process by putting it back in the hands of the riffraff.

Maybe that's not so idealistic after all:

> People-powered politics is the decentralization of power from the elites in the media, political, and activism establishments to regular people. Media access and ownership is no longer restricted to the wealthy and connected. Politics, once the playground of machine politicians and the wealthy, is increasingly open to nontraditional candidates, while supporters can now do far more to advocate and support their favorite candidates than volunteer to lick envelopes. And political activism, once the domain of professional organizers and established organizations, has been democratized by new technologies.
>
> Just as significantly, power once concentrated in the political and media centers of this country—Washington D.C., New York City, and Los Angeles—has bled out to the rest

of the country. Geography is no longer an impediment to participation, as new technologies and the shifting media and political landscapes erase those boundaries. Anyone can participate, from anywhere in the country.[7]

We'll see how all this shakes out in the years to come. In the meantime, these are heady times for bloggers, online political commentators, and ordinary folk in the hinterlands. For independents, the power of the Internet still rests primarily in its ability to bring people together. In fact, nearly every independent voter and candidate profiled in this book is someone I found on the Web or who found me through my blogs and Web sites.[8] Even my face-to-face meetings with independents can be traced back to an initial contact made on the Internet.

The Internet is also giving rise to a new brand of political activism; during the 2006 midterm elections, some 14 million people in the United States used the Web to post their own or someone else's political commentary or audio/video files, according to Pew Research Center. I can assure you that these stats are borne out in my own experience. The ease of finding and disseminating information online has encouraged my own level of political awareness and activism, paltry though it is.

Even more Americans—37 percent of Internet users or 60 million people—accessed the Internet for political news or used e-mail to exchange information about candidates and related campaign news in 2006.[9] But we weren't exactly slouchers during the summer prior to the fall campaign season; 26 million of us went online for political news on a typical August day in 2006, some two and a half times more than the 11 million Americans who accessed online political news on a typical summer day four years earlier, prior to the 2002 midterms. Even more significantly, that figure represents 30 percent more Americans who went online for political news than in the 2004 presidential election.[10] Normally, of course, you'd expect a greater degree of interest during a presidential election, but the 2006 midterms were anything but normal; the higher level of participation shouldn't come as a surprise to anyone.

As the Pew Research Center noted following the 2006 midterms, though the candidates that year made use of new technology more than ever before, the real story of Internet impact lay elsewhere: "But thus far, the most compelling narrative about the Internet's political [impact] is not about candidates' skill with new media. Rather, it centers on stories from the grassroots: activists' use of e-mail and Web sites; small donors' contributions online; bloggers' passion to tell stories and debate issues; and amateur videographers' quest to record "gotcha" moments. Perhaps that is the most fitting contribution this technology can endow to democracy."[11]

And while the Internet clearly enables die-hard and rigid partisans to find like-minded people, thus furthering political polarization, it also accomplishes the opposite: It exposes users to a much broader and more diversified range of political thought. I don't know of a single print publication that offers significant information on a wide range of political perspectives; you'd go broke subscribing to the number of magazines you'd need to read for anything resembling the wide range of political analysis and commentary that's available on just one Web site like WatchBlog.com, which presents views from across the political spectrum.

THE YOUTH VOTE

Maybe my level of activism wouldn't be so paltry had I been born thirty years later than I was. Political activism among those in the 18 to 29 demographic is on the rise, as is voter turnout in that age group. The corresponding rise in voter turnout seems like a no-brainer, but I'm not convinced it is. Political activism takes many forms. Gen X aside,[12] younger people tend to gravitate toward traditionally Democratic concerns like social justice issues. It's entirely possible to work toward righting wrongs in that arena, experience camaraderie with Democrats, and never once cast a vote.

Despite the many highly touted voter registration initiatives among youth, until 2006, voter turnout in the 18 to 24 demographic had generally been on the decline.[13] As Mike Connery points out on MyDD.com, today the youth vote is not only increasing overall, it's also increasing in non-presidential elections in which voter turnout is comparatively small. In the 2006 midterms, according to Connery, fifty-eight national offices and eighty state offices were decided by "easily surmountable or razor-thin margins . . . In almost all of these races, the margin of victory was less than the turnout increase among young voters in that state."[14]

Connery, an outspoken Democrat, is one of the best sources I've found on information about the youth vote and insight on how to capture it. Not surprisingly, he's an advocate of reaching youth where they are, and that means online. In the Jim Webb–George Allen race that I mentioned earlier, the youth vote represented half of Webb's margin of victory, according to Connery's calculations. Webb made smart use of youth-oriented social networking sites like Facebook and MySpace and apparently made sure the George Allen "macaca" video made it to YouTube and beyond.

As fascinating as Connery's commentaries are—you really need to read his "95 Theses" post,[15] which now has a permanent place on the Web, if you want to engage the youth vote—what I find to be equally intriguing is the responses to his posts from younger voters and activists. Yes, you'll find the expected anti-

Bush jeers and the Democrats-can-do-no-wrong cheers, but you'll also discover that many young people who respond to Connery on MyDD sound a whole lot like independents. As was the case with much of the electorate in 2006, youth voted in favor of Democratic candidates (in their case, 2 to 1), but according to exit polls, their vote was more a vote *against* Bush and Iraq than *for* the Democratic Party candidates. Younger voters who see only two political options express disenchantment with both; many are becoming independents, but many more barely recognize independent status as a viable option. As Nancy Hanks discovered in her work with youth, some high school students did not realize that it was perfectly legal to register to vote as an independent. One can only hope that when they get their first voter registration forms, they read them carefully and see that "no party," or some similar wording, is right there on those very legal forms.

Interestingly, though, even as Connery encourages the use of new technology to reach a technologically savvy generation, he also recognizes the value of traditional networking. After citing the value of online tools in several 2006 campaigns, he made this observation: "Overall, though, campaigns found that while this [online social networking] was an excellent tactic to energize and engage supporters, it didn't really bring new people into the campaign or help sway undecided voters. For that, grassroots, peer to peer contacts on the ground still remained the best tactic."[16]

Jackie Salit couldn't agree more. About 25 percent of the people who have become active in the independent movement in recent years have done so because they discovered CUIP and its independent voter networks on the Internet. But that means that the majority have come into the movement through traditional means, largely through personal contact.

"To me, this is an important principle of our organizing

model," Salit said, in a July 2007 author interview. "There's a tendency, given the popularity of the Internet and the tremendous force it has as a communicating device, to think that you can create new kinds of organizations based on new constituencies and new concepts overnight through the Internet. You can't."

Salit recognizes the Internet can be a valuable tool and considers it especially helpful to issues-oriented movements like MoveOn.org in rallying support. "That's a different kind of thing than the independent movement is, which is a movement for structural, political reform that's seeking to empower a disenfranchised and under-recognized constituency," she says. "Person-to-person contact, where you have independents talking to other independents on the phone, in their homes, in their communities—that tactile aspect of the organizing process is very important when you're creating something that's as out of the box as the independent movement is."

Some youth-oriented organizations have found that to be true as well; in addition to using the Internet, they're utilizing the more personal approaches of phone banking and door-to-door canvassing in order to mobilize young people to political action, according to the *Boston Globe*.[17]

And then there's that perfect marriage of online contact and face-to-face encounters, Meetup.com. Want to find other folk who are just as fed up with partisan politics as you are? Enter terms like "independent politics" or "nonpartisan politics" into the Meetup search engine along with your zip code, and you just may find a political group to your liking. Here are some of the political groups I've found that encourage political discussion from all points of view:

- The Denver Independent Voters Meetup Group issues this invitation: "Meet some of the 35% of Americans whose political views aren't dictated by any one party's platform and consider themselves Independent voters. Let's exchange ideas and opinions and have some fun while we develop ways to make a difference."

- The New Orleans Political Café, whose organizer says he welcomes political junkies; thirteen presumed political junkies joined in the group's first few months.
- The "No More Politics As Usual" Meetup Group in Phoenix, Arizona, whose twenty-four members responded to this plea: "Are you as fed up with the bickering and backbiting as I am? Let's get together and figure out what we can do to change it—and take back our country from those who are ignoring our voices."
- The Long Beach Young Adult Political Discussion Group is pretty much self-explanatory, unless you don't know that we're talking here about Long Beach, California, and you need that explained to you.
- Up the coast a bit is the IndependentVoice.org Meetup Group in San Francisco: "Independents are organizing to change the way we do politics in America—to oppose special-interest corruption and partisanship, and open the political process for ordinary Americans. Come join us and get involved in the independent movement."
- The Indianapolis God's Politics Discussion Group, where the conversation focuses on Jim Wallis's book *God's Politics*: "Come and unashamedly relish in the forbidden. God and politics! Share your joy! Meet other Independent Christians! Feel the love! Lead the way. Start the fire!"

So far, my personal experience with Meetups has been confined to knitting groups, which are held pretty much everywhere. Political groups are another matter; there aren't any in the semirural area where I live, and no, I'm not even thinking about starting one. As I said, my level of political activism is paltry at best.

REDEEMING POLITICS

If you're politically active and under, say, thirty-five, you've probably never heard of the voter education effort known as Rock the Vote. Supported by some of the most popular recording artists in the country, Rock the Vote hosts concerts and other events designed to encourage voter registration among youth. In 2003, an Alabama physician realized that Christian concerts provided an equally significant venue for reaching youth and founded a group known as Redeem the Vote. But before you understandably assume that this movement is a reaction against Rock the Vote, you need to know that the two groups have worked together to encourage young people to register to vote. It's not a movement *against* but a movement *for*.

Through the nonpartisan organization's events and Web site (www.redeemthevote.com), founder Randy Brinson also hopes to get young people more active in politics across the board. The organization was responsible for registering 79,000 new voters in 2006, but to Brinson, that's a first step. What he'd like to see next is young people of faith taking a prominent role in public life.

The group's Web site has a lot to offer in terms of voter education and all that, but I also appreciate the links to faith and politics blogs, like Talk to Action (www.talk2action.org), "Reclaiming Citizenship, History, and Faith"; Peter Levine's Blog for Civic Renewal (www.peterlevine.ws/mt); the Christian Alliance for Progress (www.christianalliance.org), "The Movement to Reclaim Christianity and Transform American Politics"; and Faith in Public Life (http://blog.faithinpubliclife.org), "A

Resource Center for Justice and the Common Good." These blogs and many, many others help evangelicals who are becoming politically active to finally feel as if they are not alone in their disenchantment with the Republican Party's takeover of an entire segment of the Christian church. For conservative evangelicals, La Shawn Barber's Corner (http://lashawnbarber. com/) provides a perspective that resonates with many in that constituency. Barber, who describes herself as an independent conservative and emphasizes that she is *not* a Republican or a Democrat, has become such an influential blogger that she even appeared on *The Daily Show*. Need I say more?

But back to one of those Redeem the Vote links. Faith in Public Life is one faith-oriented organization that has made effective use of new technology in bringing together religious groups that focus on issues like immigration, the environment, poverty, racial discrimination, and human rights. The group's "Mapping Faith" project resulted in an interactive map that identifies three thousand such groups representing evangelicals, mainline Protestants, African-American congregations, and Roman Catholics, as well as Jewish, interfaith, and ecumenical groups. Mapping Faith's research also disputed the notion of a red-blue state divide along religious lines; the resulting organizations were almost equally split among traditionally Republican and Democratic states,[18] which as we know are mostly purple anyway.

ORDINARY PEOPLE

We don't know where new technology will take us in the future. For now, the Internet provides ordinary people with access to the political process in ways they would not otherwise have had. It empowers the formerly powerless and brings into the political discourse the formerly marginalized. We can only hope that it will someday help bring about the political reform that this country so greatly needs.

I interviewed Nancy Hanks in August 2007. I'll let her have the last word on this:

> Who are we as a nation? Our history is very conflicted and rife with contradictions. If the American people can be heard, I think we will hear a resounding "Let the people decide." How can that voice be heard? I think we see that in the continuing outrage that is expressed by ordinary people on the Internet and in small and big ways across the country. I'm optimistic that the Internet will allow more people to be heard as individuals. The question remains as to whether we can leverage that into a collective voice.

PROFILE OF AN INDEPENDENT VOTER

David Cherry, 46, Chicago, Illinois

GROWING UP AS a Christian, David Cherry says he was always concerned about the plight of people who are suffering in America. That concern was coupled with his outrage over the deadly consequences of the failed politics of the Democratic and Republican parties in the African-American and poor and working-class communities.

"Too many Democrats and Republicans are only concerned about winning elections, regardless of whether their victories result in helping anybody," says Cherry. "I think it's more important to have principles and to stand up for ordinary people regardless of the outcome of an election."

An independent who has never been aligned with either major party, Cherry heads up United Independents of Illinois, a network of independent voters based in Chicago. He's also the program director for Chicago All Stars, a youth program.

Cherry says he became an independent to help develop a positive alternative to the major parties. He has no interest in running for political office but admires and supports independents who do choose to run. And while he thinks it would be great to elect independents to public office, he's more concerned about political reform—the way we conduct elections and do politics in this country. He keeps his focus on issues like ballot access, nonpartisan elections, and opening up debates on the local, county, state, and national levels. It is up to independents, he believes, to raise these issues.

"I believe that the success of building the independent political movement will determine what type of future we will have as a society," he says. "We independents are the people who are most concerned about our nation and our planet as a whole. Too many partisan politicians have no hesitation in dividing people along racial, gender, economic, and other lines if it results in getting themselves and other members of their parties elected to public office."

PROFILE OF AN INDEPENDENT CANDIDATE

Emily Lewy, 65, Dahlonega, Georgia

EMILY LEWY would like to see "none of the above" included as an option on every ballot. If "none of the above" won, the 65-year-old lawyer says, it would force a runoff election—which just might encourage the parties to do a better job.

Throughout her life, Lewy has voted in every election—even when the choices left her cold. "I often leave blanks on my ballot because I don't like either candidate," Lewy says. "I do not hesitate to vote for a candidate who doesn't have a chance, as a way of expressing my disapproval of the candidates who will be elected."

Lewy's frustration with the major parties led her to become an independent and a candidate for public office. Her 1998 campaign for a seat in the Georgia House of Representatives forced a change in Georgia election law, but not until Lewy and another candidate were disqualified from running due to a little-known state law.

"I followed the requirements to the letter and turned in my petitions a day early, not willing to take a chance on some mishap that last day," she says. "A few days later, I received a call [indicating] that my petition had been disqualified."

The information she'd been given failed to disclose a requirement created by Georgia case law: Any notary who participated in a candidate's campaign was disqualified from notarizing the collector's affidavits on the back of any page in that petition. Lewy's petition was found to be eight signatures short of the required amount because her signature, on the affidavit of some pages that she collected, was notarized by a notary who had also collected signatures. Georgia notaries were not informed of the requirement. "Neither I nor any other lawyer would have discovered it by any reasonable review of case law," Lewy adds.

Lewy filed an appeal in Superior Court, arguing that the secretary of state had a statutory obligation to provide a candidate with all information required to get on the ballot. The judge ruled against her, so she appealed to the Georgia Supreme Court. Meanwhile, her campaign was on hold ("You can't start much of a campaign when your candidacy is in question," she points out). Her appeal was denied right before Election Day.

Meanwhile, an Atlanta elections supervisor learned of Lewy's case and disqualified a County Commission candidate whose petitions she had planned to approve. The publicity about both candidates' cases prompted the Georgia State Legislature to later pass a law requiring that notice of the notary limitation be provided to all petition candidates.

Two years later, Lewy supported a candidate who would introduce legislation to change Lumpkin County's antiquated "sole commissioner" form of government. Working with the new representative, Lewy composed a bill to accomplish what she intended all along: create a five-member county board of commissioners to replace the ineffective sole commissioner. Two years after that, in 2002, the bill was passed. The following year, Lewy ran for mayor of Dahlonega and for chairman of the newly created county board of commissioners in 2004. She lost both races.

Today Lewy maintains a Web site, www.LumpkinSunshine.com, and writes an accompanying newsletter, *The Sunshine Observer,* both of which resulted from a private meeting of elected city and county officials that violated the state's Open Records Law.

And Lewy continues to beat the independent drum. "The existing system is clearly flawed," she says. "We get a ballot with no real choices. The right to vote has no meaning when there is no choice on your ballot . . . Where is a Ross Perot when we need him?" ✦

PROFILE OF AN INDEPENDENT VOTER

Jerome Holden, 43, Wolfeboro, New Hampshire

JEROME HOLDEN says he was born a Republican and figured he'd always be one. But then along came Ross Perot, and Holden realized that "this guy knows what he's doing." Impressed that Perot was able to do things he didn't think could be done by someone outside the two major parties—like participate in the debates—Holden got involved in Perot's 1992 campaign and became one of the leaders of New Hampshire's Reform Party.

Holden also became involved in COFOE, the Coalition for Free and Open Elections, an activist group started by ballot access expert Richard Winger. COFOE's New Hampshire coordinator is a state legislator—and a Libertarian—who keeps the state's 44 percent of independent voters informed about bills that affect voter rights and ballot access requirements. "That's basically what COFOE does when there aren't any elections," Holden said. "We're watching all the terrible laws that they're trying to put up to block independents from getting in."

One of those terrible laws was the infamous HB 154, which would have impacted independent voters' participation in partisan primaries. That was defeated but was resurrected as HB 194 in a subsequent session of the state legislature. "That's what they do," Holden said. "They wait till you're sleeping, and then they try to put these things through. You have to always be vigilant. But there are worse things going on that they're putting past us every day. People don't see those things because of distractions like the Iraq War. They put your focus on that and flip other things past you, and nobody even notices."

During the Perot campaign, Holden came face-to-face with petitioning requirements that consume so much of an independent campaign's time and resources. Holden and other Reform Party members set up booths at county fairs and traveled throughout the state attempting to acquire the 70,000 signatures that were required for an independent candidate to get his or her name on the ballot at that time. That figure represented 4 percent of the people who had voted in the previous governor's race; Holden participated in a series of efforts to get the requirement thrown out or reduced to 1 to 3 percent.

"I had five different parties represented in the room, and they still didn't listen to us," Holden said. "It was disturbing and disgusting. I feel like I've never been able to win any issue that I've tried except HB 154, and that we won the first time because the Democrats needed our vote. This year [2007] both the Democrats and Republicans finally are seeing that they need us."

Holden considers the petition requirements to be onerous, but there's an upside to the process. "It does get you out there and talking to people, and that gets you more support," he says. "But the problem is you're spending all your time petitioning, and you don't have time to fundraise, so you can't get on TV. The very worst roadblock for independents, or any candidate who is not one of the leaders, is the corrupt political debate commission.

"If Ross Perot could have gotten in the debates again, he would have won. If you could get Ralph Nader in those debates, at least you could get some substantive questions and answers. You wouldn't get the rehearsed answers that they always give because two of them already know what they're going to ask each other. They don't ever bring up a solid issue, and they don't ever give an opinion or take a stand on anything. It's a waste of time to watch the debates."

Holden has never run for office and never intends to, and he's not shy about stating why that is: "I don't like politicians," Holden says when asked if he's ever run for office. "I don't want to be one, I don't want to be around the lies, and I don't like the part where you have to give up other things you believe in to get the one thing you *really* believe in."

★

Chapter Six

The Pew Distrust

★

*Jesus never allowed himself to be defined by the
political conflicts of the day, and neither should we.*[1]
—Gregory A. Boyd
　　Author, pastor, and theologian

ack in the fall of 2004, as I was apparently being pegged
a Democrat simply by my presence at a particular prayer
center in the Southeast, the pastor of a church in Minnesota was experiencing the aftermath of a sermon series he had
preached that spring. The man had the audacity to speak out
against partisan politics in the church.

Like so many other evangelical pastors, Dr. Greg Boyd had
been asked to distribute political literature and petitions and
announce upcoming political events—and in so doing align his
congregation, the five thousand members of the Woodland Hills
Church in St. Paul, with the Religious Right. With the support
of the church board, he denied every request, and that rankled
some church members. So Boyd, a former theology professor
who presumably knows his stuff,[2] decided to preach on the dan-
gers of the church becoming so closely aligned with *any* political
perspective. He took a full six weeks to cover the topic to make
sure he presented the information as thoroughly and carefully
as possible.

A thousand people left the church. They chose to leave
because of their conviction that part of their mission as Chris-

tians is to openly promote those candidates who oppose abortion and gay marriage and advocate the "spread of freedom"—an expression clearly in support of the Iraq War. Boyd never suggested those convictions were not valid; he had simply warned the church against confusing the Kingdom of God with any single political—or nationalistic—persuasion. Still, some who left the church criticized him for being liberal, compromising, or, worse, a tool of Satan.

But four thousand people stayed, and had I been one of them, I imagine my frequent, uncontrollable outbursts would have turned those services into something of a Caucasian COGIC[3] experience; I don't think I could have suppressed an "Amen!" or a "Preach it, brother!" no matter how hard I tried. I've since read Boyd's book based on the sermon series and the consequences, *The Myth of a Christian Nation: How the Quest for Political Power Is Destroying the Church;* the subtitle alone was enough to convince me that this was one political book I had to read. My Pentecostal past bubbled up, and the hallelujahs just kept on coming. Greg Boyd and his kind, whoever and wherever they may be, now top my list of contemporary spiritual heroes.

America is not a Christian nation,[4] nor is it the Kingdom of God on earth. To equate America with the Kingdom of God is nothing short of idolatry, as Boyd points out. That perspective, though, is at the root of so much conservative partisan political activity that we should not be surprised when some of our religious and political leaders talk as if we live in a theocracy. We don't, but a lot of Christians seem to believe we do. They're the ones who have no problem with partisanship in the church.

I'd love to believe that the 80 percent who chose to stay in Boyd's church reflect a similar percentage among all U.S. Christians. A 2002 survey by the Pew Forum on Religion and Public Life indicated that 70 percent of Americans oppose churches endorsing candidates, but churches aren't supposed to be doing that anyway. That percentage may not apply to the broader range of political activity that Boyd's sermons and book addressed.

Within conservative evangelicalism, the notion that America is a Christian nation is a baby step away from the potentially disastrous belief that God is on our side—as long as we have conservative Christians making vital decisions that affect our domestic life and our foreign affairs. This attitude is evident "in the way political and religious conservatives vigorously and often angrily attempt to force their views and interests on everyone as if their interests, by definition, are God's interests," writes Obery Hendricks in *The Politics of Jesus*. "This is not faith; it is arrogance."[5]

Outside of evangelicalism, the problem lies not in this misguided notion that America is God's chosen nation but in the division that results—that cannot help but result—when party politics get mixed in with church life. Mainline Protestant denominations such as the United Methodist Church experience their share of partisan problems; they just don't get as much ink as the evangelicals do because they're not as powerful a voting bloc. And we all know, or should know, what happened to the U.S. Episcopal Church when its adherents were split along partisan lines in the wake of the consecration of openly gay Gene Robinson as bishop of the New Hampshire diocese. The church nearly imploded, and still may implode.

According to Cardinal Theodore E. McCarrick, former archbishop of Washington, D.C., partisan politics is also creeping into the U.S. Catholic Church, once a Democratic stronghold. "We are called to teach the truth, to correct errors, and to call one another to greater faithfulness," he told a meeting of bishops in Los Angeles in 2006. "There should be no place in the body of Christ for the brutality of partisan politics, the impugning of motives, or turning differences in pastoral judgment into fundamental disagreements on principle. . . . We don't fit the partisan categories."[6] Cardinal McCarrick's comments were part of a report on the work of the church's Task Force on Catholic Bishops and Catholic Politicians, which examined the question of whether Communion can be denied to Catholic politicians who oppose church teachings on abortion, as well as other public policy issues.

Not even the Mennonites are immune to the infiltration of partisanship. In 2005, Mennonite history professor John D. Roth proposed that the Mennonite Church take a five-year sabbatical from partisan political activity. You'd think he had suggested throwing babies against the rocks,[7] given the heated responses he got. Of the faithful, he asks: "Do we have a framework for understanding our public witness to the world in a way that regards the church—rather than the state—as the primary arena of God's active presence in history?" That's a crucial point; Roth expresses the underlying concern of those of us who want to see political partisanship removed from the church.

According to Roth, the Mennonite Church is "deeply divided" over this issue, which should give every one of us pause. If the Mennonites, who are all about peace, are forfeiting their unity over partisanship, you can see how pervasive and destructive this problem is. Roth's hope is that the church can "show a watching world that we can indeed live *in* the world in a way that confounds the logic and assumptions of the dominant culture (most of them having to do with power, coercion, and violence)" by steering clear of partisanship yet continuing to advocate for peace and justice.[8]

Daniel Vestal, executive coordinator of the Cooperative Baptist Fellowship, believes—correctly, in my humble opinion—that many Christians are looking for a radical third way of engaging in political life. That radical third way, in my not-so-humble opinion, is political independence from a faith perspective, which he inadvertently describes: "We desire to hold our Christian faith close to our hearts, but we also desire to have genuine friendship and dialogue with people of other faiths to build a human community. We desire to be involved in political decision making from our faith perspective, but we don't believe that any one party has a corner on the truth.

"We do believe that the story and truth of Scripture come from God, but we want to preserve the freedom of conscience that allows for different interpretations," he continues. "As followers of Christ we should seek to be bold witnesses, humble servants, compassionate ministers in our society. Of course this will mean engagement in the political process and public advocacy as well as prayer and worship, but not in a way that so clearly identifies the eternal Gospel of Jesus Christ with partisan politics."[9]

As Boyd writes, Jesus would not let others define him according to the political climate. Neither should we let ourselves be so defined—and neither should we allow others to try to define Jesus or Jesus-followers in that way.

THE DISINTEGRATION OF WORSHIP

While some members walked away from Boyd's church, other Christians are finding it increasingly difficult to remain in otherwise good churches, and not only because of the unspoken pressure to conform to rigid partisan thinking. What's driving them away is that the focal point of many worship services has shifted from God to government. Even if members are in complete agreement with the leadership of the church on the cultural and moral issues of the day, they're forced to sit through sermon after sermon on reclaiming America for Jesus. Any pastor worth his salt will, of course, provide a biblical basis for his political views. But that's not enough; every Sunday morning too many people across the country leave their churches without truly worshiping God. I've shared that experience with many kindred spirits, followers of Christ who, like me, wondered why on earth we continued to go to church expecting a time of communion with God; by mid-sermon we'd be flatlining, spiritually and emotionally, our hearts just too despairing to bother to try to get us going again.

Dr. Paul J. Dean, a Southern Baptist pastor in Greer, South Carolina, believes churches continue to "push politics" and provide a platform for political candidates because, as he writes on the Web site Crosswalk.com, "we refuse to see that the gospel and the worship of Almighty God may not be set aside for a party spirit, a tainted message, or a pandering politician." He goes on to ask: "When will we learn that politicians are merely courting our vote? When will we learn that very little has really changed? *Roe v. Wade* is a case in point. When will we learn that politicians promise much to obtain our vote but once elected, they go with their own political aspirations? When will we learn that there are very few statesmen left who will tell us what they believe up front and live by it regardless of the political fallout? When will we learn that we must cast a principled vote, speak the truth in love, and leave the results to God?"[10]

And that is why people like me can leave politically partisan churches in good conscience; we realize that all this political blather *is not making a difference.* I've long thought of the ineffectiveness of the Republican Revolution with regard to abortion. Evangelicals remained loyal to the GOP for decades in the fervent hope that *Roe v. Wade* would be reversed. What has that loyalty accomplished? You don't have to think very long to realize that the reward for loyalty has been nonexistent.[11]

And while pastors were preaching the Republican line, the spiritual life of their congregations was draining away, drop by drop by drop.

I've talked to evangelicals who can't put their finger on just what it was that drove them away from church. When I mention that it was the partisanship that did it for me, they look at me like I'm nuts. But I'm used to that, so I act as if my feelings haven't just been hurt for the billionth time and carry on with an explanation of what I mean by that. When I reach the point where I mention the lack of genuine worship in what we sometimes deceitfully call worship services, they get it. Well, some of them do. Others have relegated "worship" to the singing portion of the service—what has come to be known as "praise and worship" in many, if not most, evangelical church services.

The political pressure exerted in some churches is so profound that anyone who isn't on the same political page as the majority of the congregation begins to feel marginalized. It's as if you have to become what I call "born-again again." Once you're born-again into the body of Christ, you have to be born-again again into the GOP if you expect to have any hope of feeling accepted. It's not all that different in mainline churches; they just don't use the term *born-again* all that much, but the pressure to show your Democratic colors can be just as strong.

IT'S NOT JUST EVANGELICALS—FINALLY!

It's as predictable as stories about hazardous toys during the Christmas season; every election season, you'll see stories in the media about this or that group expressing outrage over Christian Coalition voter guides being distributed in evangelical churches. It's been a while since I've seen one of their guides, having managed for some time now to steer clear of churches that allow such dastardly goings-on, but I do recall the bristly sensation I'd get whenever I was handed one in a former church or two. Part of the reason for that, I'm sure, was rooted in pride; *I* didn't need anyone telling me how I should vote or where the candidates stood on the issues. In reality, most on presidential election years I had no idea who the candidates were. But I also had this sense that there was something sneaky about the whole idea of a voter guide being handed out in church. I couldn't articulate why, and not just because I didn't take the time to think it through. The fact is I didn't dare articulate why, lest I be branded a really lousy Christian or maybe even a Democrat.

What those media stories seldom pointed out is the overt partisanship in liberal churches and the even more blatant partisanship in African-American churches. No one needs me to tell them that partisanship is very much alive in churches outside evangelicalism, but I will anyway. As religion editor for a daily newspaper, I attended services at churches of every denomination in Central New Jersey, from an ultrafundamentalist, King James-only[12] church to the gay Metropolitan Community Church. At that time, in the 1970s and 1980s, political activity in evangelical churches had already been heating up, but it was just starting to catch on in African-American churches. I didn't think much of it at the time, but in retrospect I see those churches definitely crossed the IRS boundaries.

Mainline denominational churches got on the partisan bandwagon much later and much more slowly. Once they realized how much political ground they had ceded to the Religious Right, though, they began making up for lost time. In the churches I visited—and in the mainline churches I've attended in recent years—the partisan activity was carefully orchestrated and thus less likely to attract the attention of the IRS. Tony Campolo, who is often denounced by conservative evangelicals for his liberal leanings, had a far different experience: He writes of a church worship service during which members were invited to sign a petition demanding that President Bush resign.

"It is time for all of us to call upon the Election Commission to take action and put an end to any kind of partisan politics by churches, mosques, or synagogues," Campolo wrote in an online post. "And it is time for us to name the hypocrisy of the Left in complaining about how the Religious Right is violating the first amendment while turning a blind eye to their own candidates' use of churches as places to campaign."[13]

Campolo went on to defend the right of pro-life churches to speak out on the sanctity of life and of any church, mosque, or synagogue to provide a religious perspective on providing for the poor. "To live out their prophetic responsibilities, it is essential for members of the clergy to decry the outrageous happenings in such places as Darfur, and even to explain what they believe God is leading them to say about the war in Iraq," he writes. "But when the clergy start telling their members how to vote or putting out voter guides that overtly make one political party the incarnation of evil and the other the 'God' party, something has gone wrong in the land. Such clergy members and their churches should be made to suffer the consequences of such actions."[14]

The consequences are clear, although the enforcement of the law is neither frequent nor consistent: Religious organizations that cross the line face the threat of having their nonprofit status revoked or fines levied against them.[15] What's not so clear to some religious leaders is where that line is drawn, and they become incensed at the prospect of their freedom being eroded. Liberal groups like Americans United for Separation of Church and State say there's no question about where the line is; federal tax law restricts all 501(c)(3) nonprofits—not just religious organizations—from using their resources for partisan campaigns and from endorsing or opposing specific candidates.

That's it; nonprofits are free to speak out on public policy issues, legislation, ballot initiatives, and so forth, and hold voter registration drives and similar election-oriented activities. Contrary to what some religious leaders fear, tax law does not deny them their free speech rights, though, frankly, some of us wish it did. Really, pastors have a whole lot of latitude in what they can talk about and no limits on how often they can talk about it or how long they can talk about it or how many parishioners they can leave comatose in the process. And despite some churches' fears, long-time Republican activist David Barton, an evangelical, doesn't know of any churches that have lost their tax-exempt status in the last twenty years.[16]

But back to the voter guides, and one of my favorite quotes from Bob Edgar's *Middle Church:* "Whatever else the faults of the religious right may be, you have to admire the fear and respect they strike in the hearts of elected officials, many of whom dread nothing more than ending up on the wrong side of a Christian Coalition congressional scorecard."[17] Edgar has a lot to say about the issues those guides address, starting with the fact that federal firearms registration and abolishing the estate tax made the cut while "feeding the hungry and clothing the naked" did not. "To identify an agenda as 'Christian' without so much as a nod to peace, poverty, and planet Earth is a shameful exploitation of faith. Christ did provide us with a voter guide," he continues. "It's called the Gospels, and it is replete—chapter after chapter, verse after verse—with love for the poor and concern for peace."[18]

It's not illegal for the Christian Coalition to produce those fear-inducing congressional scorecards, since it is not a 501(c)(3) and therefore has that right. But here's the rub: If a voter guide is biased toward certain candidates, churches that distribute the guide can be held liable.[19] See? I knew there was a good reason churches shouldn't have anything to do with those things.

Here are several other good reasons, in case you ever need them. Like polls, voter guides can use language that skews the facts about an incumbent's voting record or a candidate's stand on the issues. You also have to have a fair amount of trust in the organization's ability to provide accurate information. Furthermore, the criteria the guides use are significant factors unless you tend to vote according to a narrow range of issues.

The Christian Coalition has been producing voter guides for several decades, but other groups distribute them as well, most notably Redeem the Vote, which was organized as a Christian version of the youth-oriented Rock the Vote. Partnering with dozens of Christian musicians, as well as organizations like the Gospel Music Association, Redeem the Vote stages events that encourage youth participation in the electoral process. During the 2006 election season, the group produced its first voter guide, this one with a twist: Instead of asking candidates their positions on the issues, the questionnaires asked such things as which church they attend, their favorite Bible verse, the biblical character they most identify with, and so forth. Those kinds of questions, says Redeem the Vote founder Randy Brinson, give voters a glimpse into the heart of a candidate. That's something the Christian Coalition questionnaire, with its black-and-white, yes-or-no format, can't provide.

"Voters of faith are tired of shrill partisanship and are weary of wedge issues. However, a voter guide that gives a real glimpse into the heart and decision-making process of a candidate is a truer and fairer measurement of a candidate's moral position," Brinson believes. "Voters of faith certainly deserve to know where candidates stand on specific issues; however, what gets lost on many Christian voters is the very basic information of how a candidate's faith experience and spiritual walk make up their political constitution. Evangelicals and most Christians are not interested as much in partisan rhetoric as in who you are, and what makes you tick."[20]

Richard Land, president of the Southern Baptist Covention's Ethics & Religious Liberty Commission, says the ERLC provides specific guidelines to Southern Baptist churches when it comes to the distribution of voter guides, no matter who produces them. "What we say to churches is don't distribute anything that you're not absolutely confident is accurate and fair, and do not run afoul of the Internal Revenue Service code," he said. "You have to be certain that it's not just one or two issues; it has to be a broad range of issues. We have a pamphlet on sort of the dos and don'ts and how you stay within the parameters of what's permissible in the law, which are available to the churches. But what we've said is we're going to do our best not only to stay within the sidelines but to stay within the side of the hash marks, and we encourage churches to do the same thing."

Every four years the ERLC produces a document comparing the platforms of the two major-party conventions with regard to certain issues. "For instance, we don't think a balanced budget is within our purview. We don't think trade policy is within our purview," Land said. "But on the issues where we feel it is within the realm of the issues that Southern Baptists have asked us to speak to them about, we just take the Democratic Party platform and the Republican Party platform side by side on those issues that are within our purview, and we make those available online and also in print form to any churches that want them."

Pastors cross the line when they do the obvious, like endorsing specific candidates from the pulpit. But Land moves the line even further; he doesn't believe pastors in their private capacity should endorse candidates, even though the IRS considers that acceptable. Pastors are called to serve all their parishioners, according to Land, and to endorse a candidate even privately is needlessly partisan and divisive. "I have an obligation to minister to all the Southern Baptists, and it's true, four out of five of them voted for George W. Bush, but I have an obligation to that other fifth as well," he says.

Even church members have been known to cross the line—by sending their church directories to political organizations. In fact, as it turns out, in 2004 the Republican National Committee actively solicited church directories, comparing their entries to voter-registration rolls and then targeting non-voters. Feeding that perception was the bad press they got in July 2004, when it was reported that the RNC had solicited church directories from Catholic supporters in Pennsylvania. "[Ralph] Reed's network funneled directories from thousands of evangelical churches to Bush-Cheney headquarters . . . Bush-Cheney headquarters sent the names of unregistered churchgoers back to volunteers across the country, who would call their evangelical neighbors and urge them to register. Some volunteers even offered to deliver registration forms and absentee ballots. Asked how many new voters the Bush campaign registered this way, [conservative coalition director Gary] Marx estimated the figure to be 'in the range of millions.'"[21]

If I was ever able to trace a call from *any* political party or group—even an association of independents—back to my church, I would do everything in my power to track down the culprit. And if it turned out that the culprit was the church leadership, I'd find a new church. When Richard Land learned of the practice during the 2004 election season, he advised all Southern Baptist churches to put an end to it, calling it a violation of trust. I'd say that's a fair description.

Because of his position with ERLC, Land is often invited to speak in churches on political and cultural issues. When he does that, he makes certain that he emphasizes the distinction between his pastoral role and his ERLC role. He preaches sermons from the pulpit during worship services, but comes out of the pulpit and holds separate discussions on the political and cultural climate apart from the worship service.

In an author interview in August 2007, Land made another distinction that is so crucial, so vital, so essential to this whole discussion of the relationship between faith and politics in the church that it needs a book of its own. I'm going to let Land describe in his own words what he says is a mistake often made by conservatives:

> It is one thing to assert the unique truth status of the Bible, it is another thing entirely to try to accord one's understanding of those truth claims with the same authority. I understand that my understanding of the New Testament is not inerrant. God is an infinite being, and I'm a finite being, and my understanding of what the Bible teaches does not have the same authority that the Bible has. As my Baptist forebears have said on numerous occasions in their confessions, God has yet more truth to break forth from his holy word. . . . Not new truth, that's in addition to, but truth we haven't understood completely yet . . . My understanding of biblical teaching is not inerrant . . . I can never be as confident of my understanding of God's revelation as I am confident that it's God's revelation.

Can you see why Land is one of my heroes? Christians outside of evangelicalism may wonder why he felt he had to say this; don't we all realize that the Bible is subject to interpretation by mere mortals? Well, no. There are no mere mortals in evangelical leadership. No, no, forget that—what I *really* mean to say is that the mere mortals in leadership think that there's very little latitude in biblical interpretation, and their interpretation is so obviously the right one that there's no need to discuss any other. I mean, come on—it's right there in black and white! How can you not see that? The Bible is crystal clear, from Genesis to . . . okay, so maybe Revelation isn't all that crystalline, but the rest of it is! Right?

AT A CROSSROADS . . . OR AT THE FOOT OF THE CROSS?

When Jerry Falwell suddenly died in the spring of 2007, the secular and religious media alike covered his passing in the context of the aging evangelical leadership. The spokesmen for a generation of evangelicals—would soon be . . . um . . . retiring or too ill to carry on with their work. That's what they wrote, but you know what they meant. Our aging leaders would soon be joining Falwell.

That brought on a spate of stories about the evolution of evangelicalism and about evangelicals finding themselves at a crossroads and about the changing of the guard in evangelical leadership. Few media outlets got the story right. A few got portions of the story right. Let's assume I didn't read or hear every story about this, and let's say a few got the whole thing right. Here are the facts about what those who got it wrong got wrong:

- Many evangelicals stopped recognizing those aging men as leaders years ago. Except for Billy Graham. He'll always hold a special place in our hearts. We can't help it.
- It's not just younger evangelicals who are disenchanted with the old guard. I'm really, really old, and I'm less

enchanted with the old guard than plenty of evangelicals half my age are.

- The "seismic" shifts in evangelicalism—the media love earthquake analogies—have been underway for at least a decade. The first tremor was felt long before Jerry Falwell was laid to rest.
- Serious evangelical discontent with partisanship in the church has been evident for about half that time. It didn't suddenly erupt with the passing of the pastor who placed politics front and center in the church.

I have no quarrel with Falwell or any of our other religious-political leaders. I am serious when I say that I believe each of these men—along with their spouses—has done a tremendous amount of good. When you peel away their political efforts, which were significant, you find an equally significant body of work that provided physical, financial, and spiritual help to millions of people, including my own family. The problem is that we do have to peel away that top layer of political activity to see the core of good work that they accomplished. And the reputation of evangelicalism within the wider culture suffered as a result. We were seen as gay-bashing, woman-oppressing, war-supporting, anti-sex, anti-fun, anti-everything hatemongers.

That didn't sound like me or any of my evangelical friends. It didn't sound like Jesus, either, and he was the One we were supposed to be following. It took a while, but eventually I started asking questions like, *Who gave these guys the right to speak for me and my kindred evangelical spirits?*

Our leaders kept trying to convince us that we were in the middle of a war, and the culture was our enemy. For a long time, I believed them. Back in the days when we used to get mail delivered by the U.S. Postal Service, my mailbox would be filled with newsletters and fundraising appeals from Focus on the Family, the Family Research Council, Concerned Women for America, and similar organizations alerting me to yet another attempt by liberals to strip us of our freedoms as Christians.

The alerts got my attention for a while. But when nothing happened after a decade or two or three, when I realized I was just as free to worship and express my faith as I was before the first letter reached my mailbox, I began ignoring them and eventually had my name removed from all their mailing lists. The America they described was not the America I experienced. The church—the body of Christ—they purported to speak for was not the church I had signed on to. The Jesus Movement of the 1970s, the wonderfully radical and vibrant expression of faith that saved my life, had been hijacked by The (Religious) Establishment while we were looking in the other direction.

Sometime in the 1990s, we began saying "Enough!" I can tell you exactly when I personally found the courage to say "Enough!": late on a Tuesday night in January of 1998 in a club in Nashville, where I was listening to a guy on stage saying things about who we are as Christians that sounded far more like 1968—or A.D. 68—than anything I was hearing in church. His name was Leonard Sweet, and he was at the club for the launch of his latest book, *A Cup of Coffee at the Soul Cafe,* in conjunction with a Christian products trade show that I was also attending.[22] Sweet and others, most notably Brian McLaren, gave expression to what so many of us were sensing—that we were missing the whole point of our lives as followers of Christ. Their message gave rise to what is now known as the emerging church (see page 144), and that message resonated with a younger generation that had discovered that the brand of faith they inherited didn't work in the world they inherited. It also resonated with newer Christians who had come to faith after years of living in the culture that the old guard, for lack of a better term, said we were at war with. And it sure as heck resonated with ex-hippie Jesus Freaks like me who were now so old and tired that we just wanted to go and be with Jesus, until Sweet and McLaren, et al., encouraged us to give life on earth as Christians one more shot.

Meanwhile, another movement was gaining traction—a progressive evangelical movement, which overlaps with both the emerging church and the evangelical left. The evangelical left has been around since the 1970s and is most often associated with people and groups like Jim Wallis and the Sojourners organization. These three expressions of faith consider themselves to be evangelical, but they don't necessarily use that term since it's too often viewed in popular culture as gay-bashing, woman-oppressing, war-supporting, anti-sex, anti-fun, anti-everything hatemongering.

"More and more people are saying this has gone too far—the dominance of the evangelical identity by the Religious Right," McLaren told the *New York Times* in 2006. "You cannot say the word 'Jesus' . . . without having an awful lot of baggage going along with it. You can't say the word 'Christian,' and you certainly can't say the word 'evangelical' without it now raising connotations and a certain cringe factor in people. Because people think, 'Oh no, what is going to come next is homosexual bashing, or pro-war rhetoric, or complaining about 'activist judges.'"[23]

The point here is that Falwell and others were already old school in the last millennium. Though it took a while for the media and The (Religious) Establishment to catch on, many evangelicals on the ground had already been turning their attention to issues like war, genocide, poverty, injustice, AIDS, and climate change and other environmental issues. At the same time, religious leaders off the ground were bickering over whether to keep a narrow focus on abortion and same-sex marriage or expand the focus to include broader issues. Their dispute, which one media outlet called a "family fight," is essentially meaningless to evangelicals who have already moved on.

And that spills over to the political arena. A segment of the electorate that was supposed to be loyal Republicans for life is anything but.

Dallas Morning News columnist Rod Dreher made this observation to ABCNews.com: "A lot of the independents who were leaning toward Republicans are now leaning toward Democrats—especially younger voters. Republicans are out of ideas, and there's a lot of anger toward Bush regarding the Iraq War. The war made me realize the danger of being tied in as a religious voter to the Republican Party. A lot of evangelicals are also upset about all the spending. We're looking for a Messiah to save us . . . Our people aren't for Democrats. They are simply sick of Republicans."[24]

Unintentionally, in those last two sentences Dreher offered a fairly accurate description of the independent movement's evangelical constituency. They're not ready to become Democrats, but they're sick of Republicans. And now they realize the danger of having such close ties with the Republican Party.

Evangelicals may be at a crossroads, but many that I know have already come to that intersection, decided which road to take, and found themselves back at the foot of the cross—right where they started their faith journeys in the first place. It's there, seeking the wisdom of God, that they are learning all over again what matters to God and therefore what should matter to them. And it has come as no surprise to them that what matters to God is much bigger than a political party's platform.

I'll leave you with this thought from Stanley Hauerwas's classic 1989 book *Resident Aliens: Life in the Christian Colony.*

The cross is a sign of what happens when one takes God's account of reality more seriously than Caesar's. The cross stands as God's (and our) eternal no to the powers of death, as well as God's eternal yes to humanity, God's remarkable determination not to leave us to our own devices. The overriding political task of the church is to be the community of the cross.[25]

THE EMERGING CHURCH:
A SPIRITUAL HOME FOR INDEPENDENTS

OKAY, SO MAYBE that's overstating it, but if you're like me and you can't abide partisanship in the church, a postmodern-friendly expression of the Christian faith known as the emerging church may be what you're looking for.

That said, it's a movement—its leaders prefer to call it a conversation—that's difficult to define. I've found that it's easier to describe what it is not: It's not an organization, a denomination, or an association of churches; that kind of structure runs counter to emergent thinking. It's not an entity with a single doctrinal stance, though it has its roots in evangelicalism. It's not another regimented program for Christians to follow. And although it emerged in response to "church as usual," its leaders take care not to criticize those who are content with church as usual.

The movement encourages people to discover new ways of doing church and being the church, which resonates not only with the 18-to-34-year-old demographic—the first fully postmodern generation—but also with older people who find themselves to be restless in the traditional church. If you came to faith in Christ during the Jesus Movement of the 1970s, as I did, you should readily understand the emerging church. We took Luke's description of the early church in the book of Acts and tried to emulate that, and we came up with some decent alternatives (think Vineyard Fellowship and Calvary Chapel), but that's not what we really wanted. What we really wanted then is what the emerging church is actually doing now.

Some postmodern-friendly churches have sprung from an intentional and interdenominational effort, such as Cedar Ridge Community Church near Washington, D.C., whose senior pastor, Brian McLaren, is recognized as the primary voice in the conversation. Sometimes, the name of a particular church is a dead giveaway that it's part of the movement, such as Scum of the Earth in Denver. Little question that it's not, say, a Southern Baptist congregation. Many, like Solomon's Porch in Minneapolis, which meets in a living room setting in an industrial building, see themselves as an experimental community. Still others aren't really churches but ministries affiliated with traditional congregations, like The Crucible, a postmodern outreach of the huge Belmont Church in Nashville. Vintage Faith in Santa Cruz, California, Apex in Las Vegas, and Holy Joe's in London are but a few others.

What all these groups have in common is this: They believe Jesus intended his followers to interact with the culture around them, not become an alien subculture. They adhere to the ancient creeds of the church. They emphasize the visual and performing arts and acknowledge the influence pop culture has on society. As much as anything else, they believe in the communal and missional aspects of the church—the responsibility Jesus-followers have to each other and to those outside the faith. And they believe that as people draw closer to God, they draw closer to each other, despite the denominational boundaries that divide them. Emerging church evangelicals comfortably draw on the rich traditions and practices of the diverse streams of Christianity, believing that by genuinely living where their common faith intersects, they can surpass the efforts of even the most successful ecumenical programs.

Beyond that, there's not always uniformity among the beliefs and practices in the emerging church, and its adherents would have it no other way. They believe faith is a journey rather than a destination, and each community of Christians needs to find its own way of continuing on that journey. Web sites like www.emergentvillage.com and www.theooze.com provide links to partner ministries and local emergent churches.

The emerging church is in its infancy, with some leaders suggesting that it's in the earliest stages of what could prove to be a one-hundred-year-plus shift in our thinking about church. But no matter where it is on an unknown timeline, it's a welcome relief for those of us who have longed for this kind of church experience. It's inclusive, it's diverse, and it's definitely, absolutely, no-question-about-it non-partisan. Independent thinkers and independent voters should feel right at home.[26]

PROFILE OF AN INDEPENDENT CANDIDATE

John Dashler, 60, Dalton, Georgia

WHEN YOU TALK politics with John Dashler, there's one topic that's certain to come up: ballot access. That's because Dashler's independent campaign for governor in 2006 ran head-on into the nightmare that is Georgia's ballot access law. "The level of ignorance on ballot access laws is up there in the 99th percentile, particularly in the legal profession," he says. "There are no attorneys that understand the election laws, except those in the state attorney general's office."

Dashler, a retired businessman who headed up corporations in a variety of industries, believes the very existence of the independent movement is at stake unless this issue is resolved across the country. There's little point in putting together an independent organization such as CUIP, he says, if it lacks a rallying cause, such as nationwide ballot-access initiatives and formation of grassroots networks to recruit and support independent candidates.

"Ballot access has to be a primary issue for independents and all independent-thinking, independent-minded people who are fed up with the political system," Dashler says. "What's the point of deciding to run if accessing the ballot is impossible? How are we supposed to have a representative government if there isn't fair and equal access?"

To show how unfair and unequal Georgia's laws are, Dashler gets specific. Petition candidates are required to submit valid signatures equal in number to 1 percent of the registered voters in the previous election, which in his case came to just under 40,000. Because of the stringent verification process, Dashler needed 60,000 signatures, assuming that 20,000 would be invalidated. Why? Because there cannot be a single mistake in the information the signer provides. If you're registered to vote as John A. Smith and you sign a petition as John Smith, your signature is invalidated; the same is true if you live at 233 Elm Street Apartment B and you fail to include "Apartment B."

"You'd be amazed how many women will not put their date of birth down," which also invalidates the signature, he said. "On each petition sheet of fifteen names, all the signers must be from the same county. If you've got a booth at a festival, you may have petitions for a dozen counties on the counter. You're busy talking to someone, and another person comes along and signs the wrong petition. Or people sign who are not registered voters. All those signatures are invalidated."

What irritates Dashler is that the interpretation of the law—enacted by major-party legislators, of course—lands on the side of the technicalities rather than the spirit of the law. In 2006, the year Dashler attempted his run, there were about seventy petitioned candidates running for statewide offices. Only one, Helen Blocker-Adams, a candidate for state representative from Augusta, made the ballot. "Had we had these people on the ballot, we wouldn't have had two-thirds of our legislators running unchallenged," he says.

And then there are the dirty tricks, like the time Dashler was invited to participate in a town hall meeting, but then his invitation was withdrawn because, he was told, none of the other candidates had accepted. He didn't buy that, and he was then told that he could come but would only be allowed to read a brief statement. And *then,* when he showed up for the event, he was told it had been rescheduled for the night before; didn't he get the e-mail? Of course he hadn't, because it was never sent to him; he asked the organizers to show him the e-mail so he could see if his name was on it, but they refused.

Perhaps the most disgusting of all Dashler's dirty-tricks stories—and he has many—is one involving an elderly barber who had agreed to put Dashler's campaign literature and a petition in his shop. The barber also had a small church next door. "The next day, he was visited by a man in a suit representing himself as an attorney with the Republican Party," says Dashler. "He was threatened—'Remove Dashler's stuff from your shop now or you will lose the tax-exempt status of your church.' I happened to walk in two hours later. I was hand-delivering his thank-you note, even though his shop is about ninety miles away. He was shaking so badly, he said he hadn't been able to cut 'white sidewalls and flat tops.'" Dashler told him not to worry about it and removed the petition kit.

Dashler, who served with the army in Vietnam and rose to the rank of captain, came to faith late in life. A conservative evangelical Christian, he ran on a pro-life, traditional-marriage platform, but he was no two-issue candidate. His Web site, www.dashlerforgov.com, reveals a wide range of critical issues, as well as his related plans for implementing the necessary changes that he intended to address as governor.

"I would not choose to run again as an independent with these petitioning requirements," he said. "You feel the full force and power of the parties: You're totally blocked out from major media. I was blocked because I scared the daylights out of them. I wasn't some fly-by-night eccentric; I took this very seriously. But by blocking me, they never had to address the fact that I existed." ★

PROFILE OF AN INDEPENDENT VOTER

Larry Reinsch, 48, Ames, Iowa

SOME CRITICS SAY "independent conservatives" are just Republicans in disguise. Critics, meet Larry Reinsch, a conservative independent who cannot imagine voting for a Democrat and very rarely has voted for a Republican. A lifelong independent, he has voted only for independent or third-party candidates since he was in his twenties. He describes independent voters as "the 40 percent of the voting public that has intellectually matured out of the two parties."

"These two parties are not giving us what we need," Reinsch says. He voted for Ross Perot twice and helped Ralph Nader get on the ballot in Iowa in 2004 but voted for Michael Peroutka of the Constitution Party, who ran on a platform of "God, Family, and Republic."

Reinsch's girlfriend, Belinda Lawler, became an independent after witnessing election abuse by the Democratic Party. She had volunteered to be a ballot courier, and then, as Election Day drew nearer, she was asked to make phone calls reminding people to vote. The script that the Democratic Party had provided volunteers making the calls indicated twice that the volunteers should tell voters to vote a straight Democratic ticket. That's "polling-place electioneering, and that's illegal," says Reinsch, who at the time we spoke was planning to file a complaint with the Iowa Election Board.

For the first time ever, Reinsch planned to vote in the Iowa caucus in 2008—which meant he had to register as a Republican or Democrat, depending on which caucus he wanted to vote in. "I get a hypocritical feeling about that, but on the other hand it's the only way independents can participate in those things," he says. The day after the caucus, voters may reregister as independents.

Reinsch, a metal fabricator who serves as state organizer for Independent Voters of Iowa, sees several benefits in the earlier primaries in 2008: "It's going to give this country more time to look at the two idiots that the Republican and Democratic parties put up. It's going to give a lot of time to say, 'We don't like these two people.' And it's going to give independents and third-party candidates more time to get to know who they're battling."

Reinsch is working to launch the Iowa Citizens' Debate Commission in affiliation with the national Citizens' Debate Commission, a grassroots effort that is attempting to abolish and supplant the bipartisan Commission on Presidential Debates. "Their [the CDC] premise is to guarantee the survival of the two-party system and to exclude third-party candidates," he believes. "The only time third-party candidates can participate is if they will help a major-party candidate look better."

Though he's not proabortion, Reinsch believes the abortion issue is being used to divert voters' attention from other important issues. "Our political system isn't working the way our founding fathers intended it to," he says. "They wanted our country to be ruled by Christian principles, but they did not want powerful churches dictating policy and agenda, and that's what's happening now."

"People say you're wasting your vote if you don't vote for a Republican or a Democrat. I believe it's exactly the opposite; you're wasting your vote if you vote for a Democrat or Republican," he says. "I say, don't vote for the candidate you think can win; vote for the one you think is the very best candidate. If people do that, we'll get better candidates."

Many conservative candidates, he says, think independents are liberals or nonvoters. "I tell them they're wrong. There are many independent conservatives who are tired of our country not following the constitutional line that was set forth for us over two hundred years ago."

PROFILE OF AN INDEPENDENT VOTER

Linda Curtis, 56, Bastrop, Texas

LINDA CURTIS launched her political life with a vote of George McGovern in 1972 to protest the Vietnam War. Since then, she's voted mostly for independent or third-party candidates, often for candidates she actively supported. Twice she ran for city council in Austin, Texas. As an activist independent for twenty-seven years, she has worked in twenty states and is now "kicking up a storm" in Texas. In 2001, following the implosion of the remnants of Ross Perot's Reform Party, she founded Independent Texans (http://indytexans.org), a movement without a party that she describes as a "big populist tent."

As an activist, Curtis works to vote independents into office, encourage discussion about issues the two major parties ignore, bring about political reform, and "help citizens fight to take back their government from various special interests who are taking a lot from the citizenry right now. We're way overdue for the rebellion that Thomas Jefferson talked about that is necessary to preserve democracy," she says, citing a letter in which Jefferson asked: "What country can preserve its liberties, if its rulers are not warned from time to time, that this people preserve the spirit of resistance?"

Curtis says Independent Texans is focused on "running candidates and ballot measures that will help win recognition, and more organization on the ground, for independents. Whether we win or lose, that's the goal—to increase the level of organization of indies." Through the organization, Curtis also promotes her pet issue: the initiative, referendum, and recall process, which she considers the most important political tools for independents: "I&R [initiative and referendum] will get you the other reforms you want. I'm very keen on teaching people what they need to know about how to conduct a fight, on the ground, against the forces of corruption."

As a paid political organizer, Curtis recently fought Austin's plans to give $120 million in tax incentives to a high-end mall by organizing small businesses to petition the city to block the effort. If necessary, she is prepared to place an initiative on the ballot to let the voters decide.

She describes the independent movement in her state as "Texas populism"—grassroots democracy that serves ordinary people rather than the party machinery. "We span the spectrum from to the right of Attila the Hun to the left of Vladimir Lenin and all points in between," she says of the ideologies represented in the hybrid movement. "We vote in either party primary. We're Libertarians; we're Greens; we're Constitutionists. But the vast majority of us simply identify as independents with a small *i*."

"What does it mean to be an independent? I think we are defining what it means, by the very activity in which we're engaged," Curtis told a 2007 political conference. "I think of us as corruption-busters . . . But there's got to be much more happening at once. We have to become politically educated and astute and much better organized. We need to learn how things work—or how they don't work, more often than not these days."

As for the 2008 election, Curtis wasn't enthusiastic about the front-runners in the summer of 2007, though she felt some of the long shots like Mike Gravel, Dennis Kucinich, and Ron Paul were "running interesting campaigns, because they're speaking out for more ordinary Americans and to independent voters. We may wind up supporting them in the primaries and see what happens in the general election," she said, adding that an independent candidate could gain the Independent Texans' support, as could Barack Obama if he "moves more independently." "It's a very fluid situation," she added. ▪

✳

Chapter Seven

Our Two-Issue System

✳

*There are times in politics when you must be on the
right side and lose.*
—John Kenneth Galbraith
    Economist

nyone who a) has attended a conservative church at
any time since the 1970s and b) did not sleep through
every sermon has likely been exposed to preaching on
a number of moral, cultural, and political issues. Some—like
school vouchers, prayer and Bible reading in schools, free (religious) speech in the workplace and beyond—are what I consider "niche" issues; some churches focus on them, others don't
give them much attention at all, and in other churches those
issues surface in cycles, depending on whatever related court
decision or legislative action is in the news. But two biggies
eclipse all other moral issues. I speak, of course, of abortion and
gay marriage.[1]

Let me stop right here and say something that needs saying:
I'm a freedom freak. I believe everyone has the right to speak up
about their beliefs and influence others regarding those beliefs,
from Focus on the Family founder James Dobson to Feminist
Majority founder Eleanor Smeal, from pro-life Senator Sam
Brownback to pro-choice Senator Chuck Schumer, from gay-
marriage opponent and former Massachusetts Governor Mitt
Romney to gay-marriage supporter and current Massachusetts

Governor Deval Patrick. Furthermore, I believe religion—or better, faith—and politics cannot be separated, at least not on a personal level. If your faith does not in some way influence your political perspective and voting choices, that doesn't say much for your faith.

That said, I confess that I do draw a line or two when the religious or political leader's freedom of expression gets stuck in a rut so deep that there's just no prying them out of it. That's when I exercise my freedom and leave those leaders to sink ever deeper into the swampland they've become mired in. I've walked away from churches where opposition to abortion and gay marriage has unimaginably succeeded in overshadowing Jesus and the awesome message of the gospel. And I've walked away from two political parties that have tried to use abortion and gay marriage not only to polarize the electorate but also to distract the electorate from realizing how little they are actually accomplishing.

Let's look at these two issues and see why neither our pastors (some of them) nor our politicians (most of them) just don't seem to get it.

THE GREAT ABORTION DEBATE

Back in the early 1970s, when the charismatic movement was just catching fire, I reported on a conference coordinated by several Protestant and Catholic leaders in the Northeast. Somewhere in the Ford Archives are my notes from that conference and in them the name of a priest who spoke about his devotion to Mary, the mother of Jesus. "I'm not asking you to understand how I feel about Mary," he said to a small group of Protestants in a breakout session. "I'm only asking that you understand that I have feelings about Mary that you can't understand, and accept that difference between us." You could hear the unspoken plea in his voice: *Please,* please *understand that this is important to me even if you don't understand it.*

I wish we could silence the abortion debate enough to hear the pleading whispers of so many women for whom abortion is a profound and heart-wrenching spiritual matter. They are silently crying out, *Please,* please *understand that this is important to me even if you don't understand it.* The women I know, both in church and out, exist along a continuum of beliefs and attitudes toward abortion, but on a political level, the debate is reduced to an either-or shouting match. What so many observers of this debate don't realize is that many who oppose abortion have come by their convictions honestly and not through the persuasive rhetoric of an evangelical leader or a papal edict from Rome. And many who support abortion have come by their convictions just as honestly, often through personal experience. I'm talking here about women (I can't recall ever discussing abortion on a personal level with a man) whose conscience—not a religious leader—tells them abortion is wrong, and women whose conscience—not NARAL[2] or Planned Parenthood—tells them abortion is a difficult solution to a difficult situation.

Because I've spent most of my adult life in evangelical churches, I understand the way evangelical women think about abortion, and though they are almost universally pro-life, they are far more compassionate on the subject than our more strident and vocal evangelical leaders would have people think. Actually, I believe some of those more strident and vocal leaders are also a lot more compassionate on the issue than they get credit for, but that's another matter. Maybe they avoid showing their compassion so they won't appear soft on abortion. I don't know.

I do wish some of our evangelical pastors would come down into the pews (I mean folding chairs; only mainline churches have pews, right?) and sit next to a woman who has had an abortion. Finding her will be difficult only because she has kept this shameful secret to herself; believe me, she's out there, dying inside a little more every time the "A" word is mentioned. And then I'd like someone to pipe in the pastor's last sermon on abortion. I'd like him to hear that sermon from the perspective of a woman in the pew who is trying so hard to be a "good Christian" that she stifles a scream every time she experiences the pain of being called a murderer—a baby-killer.

Also sitting on those faux-pew seats are mothers whose daughters have had abortions—evangelical, pro-life mothers whose daughters once gave their hearts to Jesus and led the youth group and pledged to remain virgins until they married. Those mothers also die a little inside.

The tears of evangelical women who have had personal experience with abortion could flood Death Valley. I'm certain of that.

Just ask Lois Cunningham. Cunningham, director of crisis pregnancy outreach for the Center for Bioethical Reform, in Lake Forest, California, estimates that 18 percent of the total number of women who have abortions every year—about 234,000 women—are evangelicals. That's an astonishing figure, by anyone's reckoning. It's difficult to know how many evangelical churches exist in the United States, since some choose not to be affiliated with larger associations. But let's look at stats from two of the major evangelical groups. About 45,000 individual churches are represented by the National Association of Evangelicals (NAE), and another 41,000 belong to the Southern Baptist Convention (which is not a member of the NAE). If those churches had the same number of congregants—which, of course, they don't—that would mean nearly three women in each church will have an abortion this year. That's assuming those women are still in the church. It's not unlikely that many have left, out of shame or hurt or anger. Or all three.

"The '18 percent of aborting women are evangelicals' statistic may even be higher," Cunningham told writer Nancy Hird for a *Moody Magazine* article titled "Abortion in the Church: The Untold Story." "I think there is more pressure for Christians to abort than in secular society. In secular society there is not a lot of shame involved about sleeping with your boyfriend or in having a child out of wedlock."[3]

Now *that* should give evangelicals pause. More pressure on Christians to abort? We're living in a bizarre alternate reality, it seems. There's clearly a disconnect of major proportions here.

I stand by my assertion that the tears of evangelical women could flood Death Valley. Only now I'm adding the Grand Canyon to that image.

"Becky," whose real name is lost in one of those areas of my brain that I can no longer access, literally wept whenever the subject of abortion came up. Her eyes would fill with tears that would spill over and run down her cheeks, even as she kept a steady gaze on whomever she was talking with. I knew her only briefly and not very well; we lived in the same small town and often ran into each other in a park where we took our toddlers nearly every day, but we seldom saw each other apart from that environment.

I don't know if Becky's emotional response to the issue of abortion was due to a personal experience in her past. But this I do know: Becky and her husband ("Rob"?) grieved so deeply over the loss of so many unborn lives that they were known—quietly, and without any fanfare or publicity—as the couple who would adopt babies that no one else wanted. At a Catholic home for unwed mothers, pregnant women considering abortion changed their minds when the nuns told them about Becky and Rob, this amazing couple who would gladly take in and devote their lives to babies who were HIV-positive or had spina bifida or suffered from other genetic defects. The last time I saw Becky, they had adopted six such children. And these were not wealthy people. Rob was a blue-collar worker who labored long and hard to give those children a life they would not otherwise have had.

Anyone who thinks Becky and Rob chose this incredibly difficult path out of blind allegiance to the diatribes of an evangelical leader is flat-out nuts.

Abortion is not the top-down issue that some people outside the evangelical (or Catholic) fold think it is. Yes, there are pro-lifers who *do* blindly follow what they've been told without thinking it through for themselves, whether biblically, theologically, or politically, just as there are Catholics who blindly follow edicts out of Rome without thinking them through. But for many who are pro-life, abortion is a bottom-up issue—an issue that they have deep convictions about, convictions that are not at all dependent on what this or that leader has to say.

Pro-choice women miss that sense of deep conviction when all they hear in the media is that the Religious Right wants to take away *their* right to decide what to do with their own bodies.

Likewise, when they limit their listening to the powers that be, or wannabe, pro-life women miss the deep convictions of some pro-choice women about what they see as interference in their personal lives.

For those pro-choice women, the rhetoric against abortion *is* a top-down issue. In their case, the "top" is a predominantly male tier of evangelical pastors, Catholic clerics, and conservative legislators determined to run their reproductive lives. These pro-choice women—that is, the ones who are *not* blind followers of proabortion advocates—have sometimes suffered unimaginable abuse, trauma, and cruelty at the hands of the men in their lives.

Now that they've escaped, they don't want anyone, especially a man, attempting to control their lives again.

THE POLITICS OF ABORTION

My experience with abortion is merely as an observer, a listener, and once, as an enabler. In college in the 1970s, I helped a friend get an abortion. The chances that she would survive the pregnancy were not good, and even though at the time I wasn't at all religious, I felt a profound sadness and sense of loss in that situation. There was also the fear that my friend would not survive the abortion. Her physical condition was that fragile. The day of her abortion marked a turning point in my life; facing life and death issues head-on makes you grow up fast.

When it comes to the politics of abortion, I'm also a mere observer. So I'm going to turn the mike over to Melinda Henneberger, who, after the 2004 presidential election, wanted to gain an understanding of why so many traditionally Democratic women voted for George Bush. So she traveled across the country over an eighteen-month period, spoke to more than two hundred women about the issues that were most important to them, and wrote about her findings in *If They Only Listened to Us: What Women Voters Want Politicians to Hear*. The women she spoke with mentioned lots of issues that determined which way they voted, but what struck me most was how often women cited abortion as the main reason they voted Republican in 2004. Here's part of Henneberger's commentary on this phenomenon: "I'm not sure the Democrats realize how many otherwise quite liberal pro-life women, Catholics in particular, have switched parties over this issue but continue to look for a way back to the Democrats, with whom they agree on almost every other issue. These women are not just gettable, they are all but desperate to find a way home—to the point that if the party does not send a car for them, with a really respectful driver, it will have only itself to blame. Yes, it was abortion that women who were first-time defectors from the Democrats mentioned most often."[4]

As one woman told Henneberger, "I'm with the Democrats on ninety percent of the issues. But if you're pro-life, they don't even want you."[5] That attitude was echoed by numerous other women she interviewed, including one who charged that NARAL doesn't just have a voice in the Democratic Party; the organization virtually runs the party. David Kuo, former deputy director of President Bush's Office of Faith-Based and Community Initiatives, is among those who have left the Democratic Party because it had no tolerance for pro-lifers. As he writes in *Tempting Faith: An Inside Story of Political Seduction* about his postcollege job-seeking experience, "I figured I would get a job on the Hill with a pro-life Democratic congressman. I still didn't understand that the Democratic Party had largely closed itself off to people like me. When I went to interview with Democrats, I discovered they just weren't interested in someone who was pro-life."[6]

Obviously, abortion is a hot-button issue for a reason. And it's not just because Republicans keep making it one. It's also because Democrats continue to avoid dealing with it in any practical, decisive way.

Still, Henneberger also met a fair number of women who converted to the Democratic Party despite its pro-choice platform. One pro-lifer made this observation: "[Being] pro-life is just a party dress the Republicans wear, and when we found out that forty-three percent of Democrats are pro-life, too, there went my last reason." Since she made the switch, some people at her church have let her know they're praying for her, or they've remarked, "It's obvious you've lost your faith," so she does feel she's paid a price socially.[7]

She's not alone. Women often pay the price when they go against the grain of their particular church's political persuasion. It's not surprising when that happens in a partisan context, but being an independent voter can also be isolating for Christian women, largely because of the abortion issue. If you think of independents as "undecideds," then it follows that you would think they are undecided on abortion. For pro-lifers, that's just as bad as being pro-choice. I don't know a single bona fide independent who is undecided, on abortion or any other issue, but that doesn't keep us from being thought of as spineless when it comes to crucial issues. And the far-right wing assumes independents are liberals, since independents seem to be so far off to their left, which *of course* means all independents are pro-choice. Not so, but there's no convincing some people.

Just as some polls about independent voters seem to bear no relation to reality (we're really partisans at heart, they say, and Democrats at that), polls on abortion can be so poorly worded that they fail to reflect the reality of Americans' views on the issue. "Surely at a minimum . . . our enduring reluctance to acknowledge the complexity of the abortion issue has only prolonged and hardened the debate," Henneberger wrote in an op-ed piece in the *New York Times*. "Most Americans fall somewhere between the extremes of 'never' and 'no problem' when it comes to abortion."[8]

Henneberger's book and other writings on the subject of abortion reveal an America that polls can never capture. But she is, after all, an admitted liberal, which means some conservatives will never believe she could produce a well thought-out, objective, reasoned journalistic work on the subject. (To some people "journalist" is just a code word for ultra left-wing, liberal commie. I'm a journalist; I know this to be a fact. I've faced their judgment.) So I'm going to ask Henneberger to hand the microphone over to someone whose books and writings I also highly recommend—a pro-life Southern Baptist conservative.

LAND OF THE RIGHT

Richard Land is on my ever-growing list of contemporary heroes, and not just because he once appeared on *The Colbert Report*.[9] Dr. Land, a Princeton graduate who earned his doctorate at Oxford University, is president of the Ethics & Religious Liberty Commission of the Southern Baptist Convention. That sounds impressive, but you should also know that he is gracious, witty, and most generous with his time.

And he is so pro-life that he would rather not vote at all than cast a ballot for a pro-choice candidate.

Reading that last comment, you might get the impression that this guy is a real hard-liner, the kind who thunders from the pulpit about godless heathens destroying our Christian nation. That impression would be dead wrong, though. He is no hard-liner, never thunders, and doesn't even have a permanent pulpit—not a physical one, anyway. His position as president of ERLC, though, provides him with a different kind of pulpit and the opportunity to preach a different kind of message. Like this one: "What liberals and conservatives both are missing is that America has been blessed by God in unique ways—we are not just another country, but neither are we God's special people. I do not believe that America is God's chosen nation . . . We do not have 'God on our side.' We are not God's gift to the world."[10]

I'll get to Land's take on abortion in a minute, but it's important to grasp his perspective on America's relationship to God, because it is foundational to his political perspective. America is not the Kingdom of God, he writes in *The Divided States of America? What Liberals and Conservatives Are Missing in the*

God-and-Country Shouting Match! To suggest that it is amounts to nothing short of idolatry, and Land will have none of that.

That said, Land believes America has a distinct relationship with God. "I do believe from the very depths of my being that God has blessed this country in unique and special ways," Land told me in the summer of 2007. "Blessings, by definition, are undeserved and unmerited; I believe that those blessings are providential and not fortuitous. To whom much is given, much is required," he added, quoting a portion of Luke 12:48.

And while Land opposes pastors preaching overtly political sermons, he believes they have both an obligation and a responsibility to provide biblical teaching on moral values and issues such as the sanctity of life—an issue on which he believes God's perspective is clear. His preaching on the subject is apparently influential; following one of his recent pro-life sermons, the church where he serves as interim pastor voted to donate $50,000 to a nearby crisis pregnancy center, and fifty church members volunteered to donate their time to the center.

When it comes to casting ballots, Land advises others to vote their consciences. He votes his own conscience, and his conscience tells him that he can't vote for a pro-choice candidate. "That does not mean that there are not some pro-life candidates that I wouldn't vote for," he said. "If Pat Buchanan were running against Hillary Clinton for president I would have to not vote in that race unless there were a third-party alternative. I couldn't vote for Mrs. Clinton, and I couldn't vote for Pat Buchanan, because although he's pro-life, he's also an anti-Semite, which is reprehensible to me. Being pro-choice is beyond the pale, but there are other things besides being pro-life that are beyond the pale as well."

If that's the case, it's not beyond the pale that pro-lifers could vote their consciences and yet vote for a Democrat, now that the

Democrats for Life caucus in the House has fine-tuned its program to one that even ERLC supports. "We would want to do more, but we certainly support their efforts to reduce abortions by 95 percent in ten years," Land says. "I've actually had some Republicans say to me, 'But Richard, you know the Democrats will get credit for it,' and I've said, 'I don't care who gets credit for it; I want to save babies.'"

Partisanship on the issue of abortion obscures the very real problems that surface in the aftermath of the practice, not just in the lives of the patients, but also in the lives of the grief-stricken medical workers that Land has counseled, as well as fathers who had no part in the decision to abort. "No one is in a more helpless position right now than fathers are, because even if they're married, they have no say-so, which I find horrific—that a wife can abort their child and not even inform her husband. I find that appalling.

"As far as I'm concerned, abortion is the most profound moral issue of our time," Land continues. "And if one party chooses to be on the wrong side of that issue, and it thus becomes a partisan issue, that's not my fault. That's the Democratic Party's fault." On that one point, it seems that Land and Henneberger agree: If the Democrats expect to have any hope of capitalizing on the gains they made in 2006, one of their strategies must be to become more pro-life by acknowledging the pro-lifers in their midst and, according to Henneberger, treating them with the respect they've been denied for decades.

Frankly, I don't care if the Democrats capitalize on their 2006 success or if the Republicans figure out how to take advantage of their stunning combination of inaction and betrayal of the American public ever since that success. What I do care about is electing leaders who listen to the people—the mothers and fathers, the grandparents, the medical personnel—whose real lives and real stories and real pleas are buried in polls and surveys that can be manipulated to support the arguments of abortion advocates and abortion opponents alike. As E. J. Dionne Jr. writes: "Asked about abortion in the 2004 exit poll, 21 percent of voters said that it should always be legal, 34 percent that it should be legal in most cases, 26 percent that it should be illegal in most cases, and 16 percent that it should always be illegal. Viewed one way, respondents were 'pro-choice,' 55 to 42 percent. Viewed another way, 60 percent of them gravitated to a 'middle' position on abortion. There is most certainly a conflict akin to a culture war among the 37 percent of Americans—21 percent consistently pro-choice, 16 percent consistently pro-life—who were absolutely certain about where they stood on abortion."[11]

Dionne, a columnist for the *Washington Post,* sees a great deal more moderation in the abortion debate than politicians seem to recognize. "Opponents of abortion often cannot find it in themselves to condemn a woman they know who has had an abortion for a reason they understand," he writes. "Some supporters of abortion rights find the issue morally troubling nonetheless, and might never choose to have an abortion themselves."[12]

Common ground is hard to find only when those doing the looking are rigidly territorial. And there's no one more territorial than polarizing partisan politicians who serve the power of the party rather than the people they were elected to serve.

GAY UNIONS, GAY MARRIAGE

Several years ago I was engrossed in one of those late-night conversations I love so much, the kind where neither party has the energy for pretense and no subject is off-limits. Those are moments of pure bliss for me. Engage me in an intense, one-on-one discussion on the deeper issues of life, and I forget about everything else but coffee. Anyway, that night I was sharing my always-profound thoughts with a friend in her late twenties, and the conversation turned to the refreshing changes we were seeing in the church and how her generation felt comfortable asking the difficult questions older Christians stopped asking a long time ago.

"Like this one," she said. "Why is the issue of gay rights such a big deal?"

You'd have to know this young woman to understand my bewilderment that night. Of all the questions she could have asked, that's one I never expected. This True-Love-Waits[13] pro-lifer knew her stuff, evangelically speaking; she was as well-versed in conservative Christian theology as any layperson I knew. And even though she was several decades younger than I, in some ways she was more conservative than I was at the time.

We bandied the topic about but soon got off track. As I thought about our conversation later, I felt she had given me a gift—a glimpse into the way a generation of younger Christians thought about homosexuality and gay marriage. What she hinted at, and what I later learned is true of some evangelicals and much of the secular world, is that civil unions for gays— even gay marriage—are nonissues, politically speaking. They just can't get all riled up about it.

And remember, that conversation took place long before anti-gay evangelical leader Ted Haggard was outed by his occasional sex partner Mike Jones. It's not as if my friend were defending a popular leader she blindly followed. In fact, had the conversation taken place *after* news of the Haggard scandal broke, I tend to think she would have condemned him more for committing adultery than for whom he committed adultery with.

Her attitude would come as no surprise to Rod Dreher, a conservative who works for the *Dallas Morning News,* contributes to several conservative magazines, and writes the "Crunchy Con" blog on Beliefnet.com. "The young don't have a problem with gay marriage," Dreher told ABCNews.com in May 2007. "As the older conservatives die off, it's not going to be an issue anymore. It's futile to spend our time on this issue.

"Younger evangelicals are looking for something different. They are not embracing their parents' view."[14]

This is the world our evangelical leaders and conservative politicians are facing—a world in which even the true believers are having second thoughts about the moral values they inherited. So how do those who have strong moral convictions about this issue operate within this changing political and cultural landscape?

GAY GENERATION GAP?

I write and speak frequently on the topic of forgiveness. My passion for the subject is rooted in what I see as the damage that's caused by unforgiveness, toward both the person who needs to be forgiven and the one who needs to do the forgiving. So I was stunned when I received an e-mail from a man who accused me of displaying an unforgiving attitude toward homosexuals in one of my online essays.

I tried as gently as I could to assure him that I did not hold to the attitude he described and asked him to send me the link to the particular piece he had read. I wanted to see for myself what on earth had so offended him. After reading the article, I was just as puzzled as I had been before.

Meanwhile, "Dave" had also reread the piece and followed up with an apologetic e-mail. He said he had misinterpreted what I had written not because my writing wasn't clear (whew!) but because his mind wasn't clear. His thinking was clouded by his personal experience.

Dave, a baby boomer, told me that as the son of a strict fundamentalist pastor, he grew up in an atmosphere of rigid opposition to homosexuality. He inherited his parents' moral values—and their unyielding and unkind stance on moral issues.

As a parent himself, Dave had often expressed a hurtful and intolerant attitude toward gays. And then, several years ago, his teenage son admitted that he was gay.

That announcement, Dave says, presented him with the greatest challenge to his worldview and the greatest test of his faith. He is still trying to deal with the guilt he experiences every time he remembers the terrible things he said about gays before he knew of his son's sexual orientation; he cannot imagine the fear and shame and pain he has inflicted on his son over the years.

"I love my son more than life itself," Dave told me. "Having been through this, I can't understand how any parents could turn their backs and their hearts on their own children" even when the children's sexual orientation is contrary to the parents' convictions.

And then there's his son, who recoils when he hears homosexuality referred to as a hot-button issue (which, of course, I'm guilty of—because it *is* a hot-button issue, both politically and religiously). "Seth" doesn't want to be a hot-button issue; he doesn't want his life to be extremely controversial; he doesn't want to be thought of as a threat, as he put it, to "children, families, America, God, and civilization." He just wants to be himself.

It's a wonder the Seths of the world have any shred of faith left. It's got to be hard to love a God who just might hate you.

TIRESOME . . . OR TIMELESS?
I'm convinced that polls on the issue of same-sex marriage are practically useless. I've read enough exit polls from the 2004

presidential election and the 2006 midterms to reach this conclusion with no doubts whatsoever. That's because questions about same-sex marriage are so frequently combined with questions about abortion that it's impossible to tease out the gay marriage issue. In the eyes of those religionists who fear for the future of the family, those two issues *are* of a whole cloth. But when you step away from that group, you realize that many people who have strong pro-life views are fairly lukewarm when it comes to gay marriage. So when a pollster asks a voter which issue was most important in determining how he or she voted, listing "moral values (abortion, same-sex marriage, etc.)" as one of the options doesn't provide the voter with a clear enough choice.

Our friend E. J. Dionne weighs in on the problems with polling analysis with regard to gay marriage as well:

> On the question of gay marriage, the [2004] exit polls found that 25 percent of voters thought homosexuals should be able to marry legally, 35 percent favored civil unions, and 37 percent opposed any legal recognition for gay relationships. These findings could be used mischievously by either side in the argument. It can truthfully be said that 72 percent of voters opposed gay marriage. With equal truthfulness it can be said that 60 percent favored either gay marriage or civil unions.[15]

What some of our religious leaders in particular can't seem to comprehend is that even if 37 percent of voters oppose "any legal recognition for gay relationships," that's not the big issue of the day. (One 2004 poll indicated that only 2 percent of voters ranked gay marriage as the most or second-most important election issue.) There are so many other overwhelming issues of the day, such as the economy or the health-care crisis. Both of these problems affect more Americans on a daily basis than does the issue of gay marriage. It's hard for people to get incensed about a same-sex couple wanting to get married when they're worried about paying the bills or the cost of their prescriptions. There's just no emotional energy left to vent on gay couples.

And then there's the ongoing situation in Iraq. I recently moved to the Colorado Springs area, and nearly every week the city's newspaper runs a front-page story about yet another local soldier killed in Iraq. Colorado Springs isn't just an evangelical mecca; it's also home to five military installations, including Fort Carson army base, which alone has lost more than two hundred personnel in Iraq. In that context, for many readers stories about disputes over gay marriage don't measure up as an urgent read.

Traditional-family advocates disagree; to them, any newspaper article on a legislative proposal or a judicial decision on gay marriage *is* an urgent read. Here's why, according to Richard Land:

> Marriage is anything but a personal, private relationship. That is one reason the state requires a license to get married. Marriage is a social and civic institution with profound social responsibilities, obligations, and impact. Every society in human history has severely regulated who may get married to whom and under what circumstances they may dissolve the relationship, precisely because of this institution's enormous importance to the entire society. Same-sex marriage is a cultural and social issue with profound moral, social, and public policy implications.[16]

Land then goes on to point out a significant problem that is all too often lost in the abortion and same-sex marriage debates:

Roe v. Wade established the right to abortion through a judicial decision rather than through a legislative process reflecting the will of the people and thus set a precedent for using the judicial branch to circumvent the legislative branch; gay-marriage advocates know they can avoid the tougher process of legislative action by taking their case—literally—to the judicial system.[17]

Now we're getting somewhere.

Unlike those religious conservatives who fight to silence the opposition, Land invites proponents of same-sex marriage to walk *past* the courthouse, come to the public square for an open debate, state their case, and then let the people decide by electing legislators who will vote (we can only hope) according to the people's wishes. And by turning our attention to the questionable process by which law is sometimes determined, Land has stepped away from the religious aspects of the debate and adopted a broader perspective that is more appealing to secularists—something he says Christians need to learn how to do. In any issue that involves moral values, evangelical Christians have every right to articulate what they believe the Bible teaches—in this case, that homosexuality is a sin—and express their moral convictions. But when they take their convictions to the public square, Land believes they need to enter the debate with much more than what he calls the "Thus saith the Lord" approach.

Evangelical Christians who expect to influence the broader culture also need to realize that for many people, there are other issues that loom larger in their day-to-day lives than the issue of gay rights. When gas prices have topped three dollars a gallon, when the CEO of the company you've been with for twenty-five years squanders your retirement money, when a drought attributed to climate change begins killing off your cattle, when illegal immigrants all but take over your ranch on the Mexican border, when the only way you can afford your meds is to order them from Indonesia, when your child's school comes in dead last once again in every measurable area, when you know full well that people still judge you by the color of your skin—well, you can see how the issue of gay marriage is not likely to be a priority for people simply struggling to keep it all together. They're looking for political and religious leaders who will focus on helping them keep it all together.

For conservative Christians, there needs to be a way to encourage open debate on the issue of gay unions, as Richard Land suggests, without sacrificing the attention we must give to the domestic concerns I mentioned above, as well as to global concerns like AIDS, poverty, the genocide in Darfur, the unrest in Iraq, and yes, worldwide terrorism.

For open discussion to occur, however, one very difficult and very real obstacle needs to be overcome: lack of respect for people who hold differing viewpoints. Many evangelical Christians, as well as adherents of other faiths, believe that the Scriptures clearly define engaging in homosexual acts to be sin in the eyes of the God they love. To minimize that belief is to minimize their faith. At the same time, many people in mainline denominations disagree with that interpretation of Scripture. And then there are those people of faith who fall somewhere between those two views, many of whom have wrestled with this issue for years and are still not sure about God's final word on the subject.

To successfully bring all those parties to the public square for debate, in an atmosphere of openness and respect, will be a challenge in itself. Add to that the various secular viewpoints on homosexuality, and it becomes clear that this is one issue that will not be resolved easily. If the "Thus saith the Lord" approach doesn't always work effectively among Christians, you can be sure it won't work very well in the larger society. Which is why, if we are to have any hope of moving on to other pressing issues, each person in this debate, along the entire spectrum of opinion, needs to step back, take a deep breath, and respect those with opposing perspectives on the legal and moral aspects of same-sex marriage while trying to find common ground with each other on these other pressing issues wherever possible. It still won't be easy, but the animosity that has characterized so much of the debate on this issue just might begin to dissipate.

So . . . is this a tiresome debate, a moot point, with the legalization of gay marriage all but a done deal? Or is this a timeless issue, one that is crucial to the survival of societies everywhere? I tend to think the former is likely—that same-sex marriage will be legalized, due to a combination of aggressive activism by gay rights advocates, indifference on the part of the electorate, and issue-fatigue among some evangelicals and other religious conservatives who are simply tired of the rhetoric. Whether society will crumble as a result, we just don't know—and that's why the fight against gay marriage is not likely to go away in the near future, if ever. Same-sex marriage appears to be both a tiresome and a timeless issue.

PROFILE OF AN INDEPENDENT VOTER

Mark Ritter, Frankfort, Kentucky

MARK RITTER, supervisor with the Kentucky Natural Resources and Environmental Protection Cabinet, has been a registered independent since 1991. But he found himself "confused and annoyed" by a poll of attendees at a 2007 independent voter conference revealing that more than 90 percent supported open primaries or granting independents the right to vote in partisan primaries. That, to him, indicates a lack of commitment to their standing as independents. "It is not necessary for me to dilute the current political parties to enhance the credibility of my politics," he says in response.

"I registered independent because it is a comfortable fit," Ritter continues. "I could not align myself politically, and to a lesser extent socially, with staunch Republicans or Democrats." He believes partisans tend to stereotype a person based on incomplete information and their biased assumptions. Independents are perceived as "unpredictable and contradictory to their values." I'll let him take it from here; this is what he had to say about his experiences with political paradox:

I am employed by the Kentucky Department for Environmental Protection and fully devoted to the mainstream efforts of regulatory compliance. However, my ten years in industry have allowed me to empathize with the challenges of manufacturing managers. *Some career government employees tend to begrudge this relationship.*

I am an army reserve officer and currently hold the rank of major. I have been deployed in support of the current operations. I do not "hate" George Bush. I do disagree with selected policies and think he aligned himself with some seriously ill-advised decisions. *Generally, a significant percentage of Kentucky DEP employees do not assimilate easily with those serving in the military.*

I have held midlevel leadership positions with the Sierra Club. I support the recent Supreme Court decisions regarding CO_2 emissions and installing control devices at existing utilities. *It is often amusing when a Sierra Club member finds out I am currently serving in the military and vice versa.*

I attend a Presbyterian church and find the conflict between evolution and the book of Genesis to be generally ridiculous. I view parts of the Bible metaphorically, such as, "God created the heavens and the earth" in seven days, as the author's descriptive choice, not a hard fact describing seven twenty-four hour days. *Our Kentucky governor gets considerable support from hard-line Bible-thumpers. Yet, I don't want to join the agnostic granola (flakes, nuts, and fruits) crowd claiming intellectual enlightenment in lieu of Christian commitment.*

Ritter believes that people who cannot conform to the values and limitations of a particular political group need to align themselves with the independent movement—even if it means isolation. "I am frustrated that the mainstream parties are unable to resolve society's issues because their priority is developing relationships for power and wealth instead of pragmatic solutions," he says. "Idealism has merit. It just isn't what most people are about."

PROFILE OF AN INDEPENDENT VOTER

Mike Clawson, 28, Yorkville, Illinois

AS A TEENAGER, Mike Clawson was a "pretty hard-core Republican" who listened to the likes of James Dobson, Chuck Colson, and Rush Limbaugh. He briefly considered studying political science at Jerry Falwell's Liberty University but opted instead for Wheaton College, where he met progressive Christians who cared about poverty, the environment, gender equality, and similar issues.

"I started noticing how often the Bible talks about compassion and justice for the poor, and I started to question how my conservative Republican views fit with that," Clawson says. "My former pro-America stance also started changing dramatically the more I read about the Kingdom of God in Scripture and started realizing that as a Christian I owe my primary allegiance to God and not to a nation-state."

His studies in postmodern philosophy led him into what has become known as the emerging church movement. Through the emerging church's emphasis on a positive engagement with culture—rather than the traditional evangelical "culture wars" mentality—Clawson started listening to opposing viewpoints, and many of his old conservative Christian assumptions started to fall apart.

Feeling betrayed by the failure of

the Republicans to fulfill their "Contract with America" and bring about political reform, in 2000 he voted for Ralph Nader—not because he identified with the Green Party but because of the corporate control of the two major parties.

After 9/11, Clawson's disenchantment with many of Bush's policies forced him to pay closer attention to politics—and to activists in Christian social justice circles. As he learned more about fair trade, global poverty, corporations' exploitation of the poor, and political corruption, he became even more disillusioned with both major parties. "Both seemed to be just as much a part of the problem as the other. I think the Republicans, and especially neocons, are more of a danger right now and need to be stopped, but I don't hold much hope of the Democrats producing much in the way of real reform or just policies, either," he says.

Clawson serves as pastor of Via Christus Community Church, a small emerging church in Yorkville that he and his wife, Julie, started after leaving a Baptist church in Wheaton where he served as youth pastor—in part because of the senior pastor. "He thought we shouldn't give to the poor because that would be showing favoritism, and that the way to help them was to be good consumers to stimulate the economy and create jobs," he said. "He managed to bring up the war in Iraq—favorably—or the threat of gay marriage in nearly every sermon." At Via Christus, the Clawsons foster an open attitude toward diverse political and theological viewpoints.

For someone with a history of political apathy, Mike Clawson today has a laundry list of issues he feels passionate about:

- Top-to-bottom reform of the electoral system, including publicly funded elections; an independent redistricting commission; scrapping the electoral college; a balanced-budget amendment; better access for independents and third parties; and term limits, better oversight, and stiffer penalties for corruption.
- Greater focus on justice and poverty issues.
- A resolution to the war in Iraq and, more broadly, a change in American foreign policy.

"My faith calls me to stand apart from partisan politics in order to be a prophetic voice within the system. I don't believe that we as Christians should be disengaged from politics, but rather we should be 'in it, but not of it'—raising our voices and exercising what influence we have on behalf of the poor and oppressed, while at the same time eschewing the partisan power games and politics of self-interest."

PROFILE OF AN INDEPENDENT CANDIDATE

Mike Crane, 58, Fannin County, Georgia

MIKE CRANE, a computer technician, has a long and varied history of political activism, starting with the days he spent driving around Georgia in the back of a pickup as he helped put up "This is Maddox Country" signs supporting Lester Maddox's successful bid to become governor. That was in 1966 when Crane was a freshman at Georgia Tech, and he enjoyed that experience so much that he became involved in what was then the Southern Democrat wing of the Democratic Party. Over the next few years he served on county Democratic committees in Clayton County, Georgia, and Fairfax County, Virginia, and as the Georgia State Young Democrats membership director.

As the Democratic Party began changing, Crane became inactive in the party and in 1988 switched to the Republican Party, serving on several campaign steering committees and the Broward County, Florida, party committee.

After coming to the conclusion that the Republican Party, like the Democratic Party, was too embedded with special interests, Crane became one of the founders of the Southern Party in 1999. He has avoided the two major parties ever since; "I see nothing on the horizon to indicate that will change," he says.

In 2002, Crane ran for office for the first time, as a Southern Party candidate for Fannin County Commission Chairman, receiving 20 percent of the vote. In both 2004 and 2006 he was a petition candidate for Georgia State Senate District 51. "Despite gathering over 7,000 signatures, I fell victim to the hardest ballot access laws in our country and missed ballot access by about 250 signatures each campaign," he says. "But meeting and talking to roughly 8,000 fellow citizens in person has been one of the most rewarding experiences of my life."

Professionally, Crane spent most of his career in high-tech software product development, focusing on audio technology. He currently designs Web sites and develops Internet software. He and his wife, Pam, have three adult children and ten grandchildren, live in the north Georgia mountains, and belong to Morganton Baptist Church.

Crane's main political focus, as well as that of the Southern Party, is concern over the loss of America's founding principles. Government at all levels is becoming increasingly embedded with special interests, he says, and with every election cycle there is less and less competition. "After spending roughly thirty years supporting a 'lesser of two evils' mentality, for the last ten years, and for the remainder of my life, I am now working for what I believe in," he says.

That includes these issues:

- **Role of government.** The primary function of government is to protect the God-given rights of its citizens, not to determine which rights the government will allow the citizens to retain.
- **Political competition.** There is no constitutional provision at the state or federal levels for preferential treatment for Republican and Democratic parties.
- **Special interest influence.** Ending excessive special-interest influence, whether it be developers destroying the environment, corporations raiding the public treasury by tax subsidies, or organizations demanding special treatment, is necessary for a return to good government.
- **The states' check on the federal government.** The states need to be the primary check on the out-of-control federal government, as intended by the founding fathers.

Crane's choice for president in 2008 is Donnie Kennedy, not a surprising choice since he serves as the treasurer of the Walter D. ("Donnie") Kennedy GOP Presidential Exploratory Committee. "Among the rest of the candidates, probably only Ron Paul has read the Constitution in the last twenty years or so," he believes.

"Whether or not independents can have success addressing issues is in the hands of the citizens of our country," Crane says. "Success or failure is not as important to me as the fact that I am a grandfather. I am concerned about the world being left to my grandchildren. I believe that a majority of grandparents [and parents] have this concern, and in a more open political environment would elect higher quality elected officials."

★

Chapter Eight

Final Tally

★

*We've wandered into a political region in which
partisan conflict has become more intense than in
almost any other period in American history. The
transpartisan movement is beginning to foster so
much communication across the partisan boundaries
that the boundaries themselves are beginning to be
much more porous.*
—Former Vice President Al Gore

ow that I've given independent voters a generous
amount of ink, it's time to extend my generosity to
partisans. I'm taking the high road here and inviting
partisans in on the discussion, and I'm starting with an extraordinary effort that's being conducted to bring together Republicans, Democrats, independents, third-party members, liberals,
conservatives, moderates, and any other group you can think of.
But we'll turn to an independent to kick off the discussion.

Until recently, Joseph McCormick's professional resume
showed him to be a Republican through and through. A graduate of Virginia Military Institute and Yale University and a
former officer in the U.S. Army Rangers, McCormick helped
coordinate a national field campaign for Bush-Quayle '92 in his
position as assistant to David Carney, the campaign's political
director. In 1998, he decided to run for Congress, challenging
the Republican Party-backed candidate in the Georgia primary.
His win against the clear GOP favorite garnered the attention

of Republicans in Washington, and soon he was on the receiving end of help from the likes of Newt Gingrich, Senator Robert Dole, Marilyn Quayle, and Georgia senator Paul Coverdell. He lost the general election that fall but later went to Washington to join the Bush administration. "That didn't work out," McCormick told me. "The Reagan Republicans had supported me in the election, but the Bush team was a different team. I found I had made some political enemies."

Leaving Washington sent McCormick, then thirty-nine, into a classic midlife crisis. His political friends abandoned him, his wife left him, his sister—who virtually raised him—died of cancer, and his business partners tried to wrest company control from him. Discouraged and disillusioned, he retreated to a cabin in the Virginia mountains and tried to figure out who he was and what had just happened to him.

It took three years, but with the help of a new friend, McCormick began to feel whole again. Pat Spino was not the kind of person a die-hard Republican would normally befriend. She was a member of an "alternate community"—think a new-millennium version of a hippie commune—and worked as its midwife. Instead of conflicting with his conservative values, though, the group's liberal values turned out to be more like his than he expected.

In 2003, McCormick and Spino founded the Democracy in America Project, interviewed people from various political perspectives, and discovered that "We the People" were not the Republicans or the Democrats or the minor parties or even the independents, but an amalgamation of every political persuasion, including no persuasion at all. Having amassed a wealth of information as well as fresh perspectives on what it meant to be an American and what it meant to be political, McCormick became an "unaffiliated" voter. But what's more important is that he set out to change America, one conversation at a time.

DEMOCRACY IN AMERICA

In June of 2004, a remarkable group of civic and political leaders gathered at a retreat center in Michigan. Among the participants were David Keene of the American Conservative Union and Joan Blades of MoveOn.org; Ahmed Younis of the Muslim Public Affairs Council and Brenda Girton-Mitchell of the National Council of Churches; Maggie Fox of the Sierra Club and Roberta Combs of the Christian Coalition. The event was the first Democracy in America conference, and its purpose was to "reconnect a broad spectrum group of Americans to the ideals, values, and principles that represent the 'spirit of America.'"[1] Through civil dialogue focusing on what each participant was *for* rather than *against,* the group's aim was to build trust and communication across political lines.

That's a tall order, and moreover, it sounds a lot like an idealistic hugfest from the '70s. But it was such a successful, breakthrough event that a second one was held the following year, and then another, and yet another.

In one short year, McCormick and Spino, along with the organization Let's Talk America, had put together the invitation-only conference that attracted opinion leaders representing such diverse groups as the American Legion, Common Cause, Equal Rights Advocates, the League of Woman Voters, AARP, Citizens for Health, Americans for Tax Reform, *Utne* magazine—and the American Gas Association. These people were expected to participate in facilitated dialogue on unifying principles that define America *and* be civil about it, listening deeply, respecting each other's point of view, and not slugging it out even once.

The following year, the Christian Coalition and MoveOn.org cosponsored a second conference attended by leaders of organizations representing 70 million Americans. If that doesn't convince you of the success of the first conference, nothing will.

The concept behind these events, and the reason for their success, is a philosophy known as transpartisanship—a carefully chosen word that avoids the left-right connotation of bipartisanship and conveys a perspective spanning the full range of political thought. Through transpartisan dialogue—and simply getting to know each other as human beings—people began to shed their biases and preconceptions about each other and started to form relationships that outlasted the conferences.

One result of the events is the new and unexpected alliances that have cropped up between groups that were previously considered adversaries. "When you realign these coalitions, then all of a sudden the red-blue leaders have to pay attention," McCormick said. "If the Christian Coalition starts working with the liberals, then the Republican leadership has to pay attention. The same with the Democratic leadership; they can't monopolize things when these coalitions start to shift."

Sometimes, the new relationships and new coalitions exist on a stealth level. It's one thing for the leader of a liberal organization to acquire newfound respect for the leader of a conservative organization, but it's a whole other thing to expect die-hard liberal contributors to cheer on a budding friendship with a right-wing association.

But McCormick hears the rumblings, and he knows there's a lot going on beneath the radar.

"The fascinating thing that's happening is that I'm seeing the dream actually coming true," he says of the surprising relationships that are being formed. "Our political process, our red-blue process, will not tell the truth about what's really on the minds of the American people. It wants to talk about wedge issues in sound bites, and it doesn't want to talk in any depth about things people really care about. There's great anger, there's great frustration, there's great alienation from this red-blue game. Obviously, the independent movement is a reflection of that.

"We're developing coalitions of coalitions that are beginning to cooperate in ways the red-blue establishment did not expect. We have an opportunity to transform the system."

REUNITING AMERICA

A second outcome of the Democracy in America conferences was the founding of Reuniting America (www.reunitingamerica. org), a national campaign designed to promote and facilitate political reconciliation by getting Americans to reengage with each other. Michael Ostrolenk, codirector with Ana Micka, calls the group a "neutral convener," meaning that it brings together leaders from across the political spectrum while the organization itself remains politically neutral. "Reuniting America doesn't start off with taking stances," Ostrolenk told me in a May 2007 interview. "Out of the discussions that take place and developing relationships, things happen. Possibly and hopefully they can civilize the political discourse a bit. Those people who discover common ground can then move forward."

That sometimes means moving forward to work with Liberty Coalition, a policy group founded by Ostrolenk that does take stances. "We've sat with Michael Chertoff and Homeland Security, and we've sat with the FBI, and our intention is not to find space for common ground unless that common ground is protecting our constitutional rights," Ostrolenk said. "We have clear positions that we take. Our intention is to convince them that they need to do what we think is appropriate."

Liberty Coalition's transpartisan working groups focus on specific policy issues. A group that focuses on an issue such as tax reform would include individuals representing tax-oriented groups that have different political stances on taxation. "I don't think we're going to have everyone agree on everything, and if we did that would be boring," says Ostrolenk. "The tension causes new ideas to emerge. What's useful is if relationships can be developed, and people are allowed to articulate their positions in an intellectual way so that the other side or sides are able to listen deeply and try to understand the assumptions the other person's holding."

One of Ostrolenk's friends calls Liberty Coalition a "force multiplier" that compels Congress to recognize that groups across the political spectrum support a particular issue. What Ostrolenk has found is that someone from the left will seek the help of a new friend on the right to gain access to a Republican member of Congress and vice versa. "The right will come to us and say, 'We're working on this, and we think some more liberal, progressive groups might be interested in this. Can you help facilitate the connection?' and then the relationships develop over time, which is always important," Ostrolenk said.

That's all well and good, this bringing together of powerful opinion leaders to work on our country's problems and make nice with each other in the process. But what about the rest of us? Where do we come into the picture—the little people who are not leaders of powerful organizations, who have never been known as either movers or shakers except perhaps in a literal sense, who don't have much influence but would be ever so grateful if someone would listen to us anyway? Well, you'll be happy to learn, as I was, that Reuniting America promotes several programs that can get us talking to each other in the same way those leaders at their high-powered retreats get to talk to each other. There are no retreats for us at five-star resorts—yet (yes, I'm hinting)—but we have several other options, including:

- **Town hall dialogues:** These day-long events organized by Reuniting America follow a format known as "World Café." Participants sit at café tables in groups of four that allow for a more easy, relaxed conversation than you'd ever have in the typical "breakout session." *This* is my kind of meeting, if you can even call it that. You get to talk about things like the deepest longings of the American people and what you think it would take to satisfy those longings or what values you cherish and where you see them reflected in political life. Just load me up with coffee, and I could soak up that kind of conversation all day. I might even participate.
- **Conversation Café** (http://www.conversationcafe.org/): Not officially connected to Reuniting America, but the two groups link to each other and are clearly on the same wavelength. Here the conversation is generally less political, with participants talking about things like what they think the purpose of freedom is and when they feel most alive and what they think we could do to make life better right now. These events are organized by local hosts around the country.
- **Let's Talk America** ("What if what unites us is more than we realize and what divides us is less than we fear?"): A movement to get people talking—in smaller venues like cafes, bookstores, and homes—about the state of our democracy and its future. The discussions are designed to be inclusive, nonpartisan, respectful, and "new," as in creative. Like Conversation Café, the group provides training for those who want to host a conversation; you can sign up or find a group at http://www.letstalkamerica.org/.

Each of the groups above link to similar programs that foster open conversation among ordinary Americans, if there is such a thing. Some groups around the country bring together people from diverse perspectives and lifestyles to discuss the deeper issues of life and politics over a home-cooked meal, but being in one of those groups means you have to cook every now and then. The café deal is more my style.

REPRESENTING AMERICA

Finally, let's look at probably the most innovative bipartisan—or actually, transpartisan, now that I've become so accustomed to using that word—approach to presidential elections that has ever come along: Unity08. If someone had come up with this idea sooner, I can almost guarantee there wouldn't be so many independents today. Now that we're here, independents are not going away, but we are paying close attention to this creative approach to electing a president.

There's just one problem. The idea is a great one, but not so much its implementation. As of the summer of 2007, the grass-roots movement that would allow Americans to choose a presidential slate from two different parties or political factions at an online convention is embroiled in so much controversy that it seems likely to implode. Critics have charged Unity08 with fabricating its grassroots origins, failing to respond to questions about its finances and challenges to some of its claims, and refusing to reveal the names of "advocacy partners" and lobbyists who are involved. These questions aren't being asked by the media; they're being asked by Unity08 members—the very people who are supporting the effort.

For what it's worth, Republican senator Chuck Hagel of Nebraska was among those seeking the Unity08 nomination in mid 2007, though he's also been named as a possible running mate for Michael Bloomberg should he enter the race as an independent. Other likely contenders are Joe "Independent-in-Name-Only" Lieberman of Connecticut, Arizona senator John McCain, and any major-party presidential candidate who is overlooked by his or her party as the designated nominee.

But that's only if Unity08 survives the growing discontent being expressed on the Internet by those who want to know where their contributions are going.

To quote from Unity08.com: "Neither of today's major parties reflects the aspirations, concerns or will of the majority of Americans. Both parties have polarized and alienated voters. Both are unduly influenced by single-issue groups. Both are excessively dominated by money."[2] If the allegations are true, Unity08 fits its own definition of a major party.

What a bummer. We finally get something that looks so promising, and it turns out it may just be a sham. I don't know whether it's for real or not. All I know is, I sure wish it were.

Which brings us back to where we started: the independent movement. We'll probably gain a few hundred thousand more registered independents if Unity08 bites the dust.

SO . . . WHO'S THE WINNER?

Well, we are, but only if we claim the victory that is ours. We can do that by rejecting the notion that we're a hopelessly polarized nation—a notion that is in the interests of the two major parties to promote. We are not rural reds and urban blues, religious reds and secular blues, conservative reds and liberal blues. Each one of us is more complex than that, and that makes us a nation of wonderful diversity. To reduce our culture to such a false dichotomy is to limit our potential and to delay finding solutions to the problems that plague our society, many of which we ourselves created. Perpetuating division is a partisan ploy that only serves to throw more roadblocks in our way.

My involvement with the independent voter movement has given me great hope for the future of this country, hope I didn't have before. Nancy Hanks (The Hankster), expresses a similar sentiment:

> Looking at the history of the most recent American insurgent movement, from George Wallace to John Anderson to Lenora Fulani to Ross Perot to Ralph Nader, I think we can feel proud of our grassroots movement [that is] evolving from an offshoot of disgruntled Democrats and Republicans to a genuine movement of the American people to disassociate from the partisan tribes. Independents are now mainstream . . . I think that gives great hope to our country. It's independents who are leading the way to a more coherent national policy.

A coherent national policy. We can only hope—and vote, and pray, and work like crazy to make it a reality.

PROFILE OF AN INDEPENDENT VOTER

Mitch Campbell, Twin Falls, Idaho

MITCH CAMPBELL has a plan—a "government plan" for America that only independents can deliver.

"Every time I watch the news or read any news publications my attention is instantly focused on how important the independent movement is," says Campbell, who founded and heads up the American Independent Movement of Idaho. "As most Americans now realize, neither the Republican nor the Democratic Party can improve our situation. The problem is fairly broad, but to start, the primary purpose and goal of the Republican and Democratic parties is to maintain control and power."

Because of the enormous amounts of money that parties receive, contributors expect something in return, Campbell says, and that translates into legislation benefiting special-interest groups and support for only those candidates who are true party loyalists, regardless of their suitability for the job.

"If either political party introduces good legislation, the other party will attempt to defeat it or amend it so the opposing party will not receive the credit," Campbell says. "Legislation that survives the partisan assault is usually so altered and amended it barely resembles the intent or purpose of the proposed bill and more often is what special-interest groups want."

In the spring of 2007 Campbell testified before a state legislative committee on a bill that would end the state's open primary system, forcing independents to register with a major party in order to vote in that party's primary. He charged that the bill was an attempt to protect the rights of political parties while in effect disenfranchising 37 percent of the Idaho electorate—its independent voters. Campbell's testimony challenged the legislators to defend a bill that would allow the rights of political parties to prevail over the rights of individual citizens. The bill was defeated.

"Republican candidates represent the Republican Party; Democratic candidates represent the Democratic Party. Who represents you and me and the other 200 million Americans?" Campbell asks. He believes independents are largely motivated by dissatisfaction but "like the Democrats" have no plan for governing. Toward that end, Campbell and AIM have created a platform for independents so they'll be ready when their moment arrives. The platform addresses:

- Campaign finance reform
- Reform of partisan politics

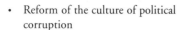

- Reform of the culture of political corruption
- Open primary elections
- Selection and election of quality candidates
- Judicial system reform
- Social Security reform
- Government finance and fiscal responsibility
- Sound foreign policy

- Comprehensive environmental policy
- Energy policy
- Restoration and preservation of civil liberties
- National health care plan.

Campbell plans to develop and publish the details of his plan for governing America in a forthcoming book.

PROFILE OF AN INDEPENDENT VOTER

Russ Ouellette, 47, Bedford, New Hampshire

AFTER EIGHTEEN YEARS working for a defense contractor and a lifetime as a Republican, Russ Ouellette's thinking began to shift toward the middle. He'd get into conversations about politics, try to articulate his perspective, and ask if someone could help him figure out what he was now that he wasn't really a Republican. No one could tell him; the best they could do was point him toward major-party politicians and a Libertarian or two in hopes that they could help him figure it out. What he discovered was that everyone he talked to was "buying into" the status quo of the political system.

Even so, he admits, "I was embarrassed. I didn't want to say I was independent."

Then two factors helped him get his bearings. First, he enrolled in a doctoral program in organizational leadership and began reading books on philosophy, sociology, and psychology related to his field.

"It dawned on me that we've been brought up in a very rational society," Ouellette says. "Business is trying to move to more open-system thinking and more empowerment, and yet all our institutions are exactly the way they were fifty years ago—which basically means that they don't work anymore. You can't build these ratio-nal structures and expect people to behave in a free and open way. It's not going to happen."

When he looked at politics through that lens, he realized that the same principles applied. "It's almost old-fashioned, in the sense that you have two constituencies and the only thing they care about is the machine that they're running," he said.

The second event was a chance meeting with Fran Miller of CUIP, who connected him with Betty Ward, a New Hampshire independent activist. Ward called Ouellette, and ninety minutes later, he knew who he was. "I felt like somebody found me that understood what I was thinking," he said. And someone who applied critical thinking to her political perspective.

"There's no critical thinking in politics," he says. "We preach it in business, we preach it in our schools, but yet for some reason in the political process critical thinking isn't part of the story. And this is why I'm an independent. Independents can add critical thinking to the process."

Until his conversation with Ward, Ouellette's only political experience was as a campaign worker—for Pat Buchanan. He admits to being a bit embarrassed when he tells people that today, though he genuinely liked Buchanan and felt he made a lot of sense on some issues. He also admired John McCain and Joe Biden for their honest perspectives. Soon enough, Ward and Miller got him involved in a battle against a primary voting rights bill that negatively affected independents. He credits Ward with doing a lot of the legwork, but he contributed by contacting legislators to urge them to vote against the bill and calling and meeting with New Hampshire residents to encourage them to do the same. "Betty went and testified, but the stuff I did was pretty cool too," he says. "They [state representatives] got to know me. They know I'm an independent, and that's cool, and they're returning my phone calls. It was like I'm someone to keep an eye on."

Ouellette's Catholicism and his work as a corporate consultant factor into his opposition to the war in Iraq. "Any first-year student of organizational development would have told this guy [President Bush] and his staff that you can't go into a culture and expect to set up a democracy," he said. "The change is too drastic. And then to draw up old policies from Vietnam and bomb Iraq and think that's going to change something to me makes no sense. Yet we get half of the Senate and half the Congress and half the country to think that that's the righteous thing to do. It doesn't sound Christian to me. It sounds old-fashioned Christian and scared, fearful Christian. What would a true Christian do? Go feed them." ✦

Notes

PREFACE, OR THE MAKING OF *WE THE PURPLE*

1. Don't pick mine.

INTRODUCTION

1. Who knows which one? All three are credited with writing and editing the magnificent *America (The Book): A Citizen's Guide to Democracy Inaction* (New York: Warner Books, 2004), 107.

2. "Bipartisan Group of Representatives Holds News Conference on Medicinal Marijuana," *Federal Document Clearing House Political Transcripts,* July 24, 2002. Quoted on http://www.wordspy.com/words/purplestate.asp and http://www.mapinc.org/drugnews/v02.n1401.a04.html and accessed November 24 and 28, 2006, respectively.

3. Thomas Fitzgerald, "Narrowing 'God Gap' Raises Eyebrows," *James Logan Courier,* December 3, 2006. Posted on http://jameslogancourier.org/index.php?itemid=1162 and accessed November 2, 2007.

CHAPTER 1: PURPLE REIGN

1. I hate the word *hippie.* I hated it then. I hate it now. I use it here only for the purpose of parallel construction and alliteration. I am a writer, after all.

2. I have no idea what this is and no inclination to find out.

3. I wish I could insert it here, but that would jack up the price of the book, and we'll have none of that. You can find the map at http://www.princeton.edu/~rvdb/JAVA/election2000/ and elsewhere on the Web if that link expires at some point.

4. This one is at http://www.princeton.edu/~rvdb/JAVA/elections/Multiyear3.gif.

5. Not to be confused with Great Britain's Purple Party, launched in 2005 by Laurence Llewelyn-Bowen, who hosted such shows as *Changing Rooms, Homefront, Fantasy Rooms,* and *Taste.* Bowen's raison d'etre is to preserve Britain's architectural heritage. Part of his party's "manifesto" provides for up to 100 percent tax relief for nominated citizens who have "performed a heroic, generous, or selfless act." Woe to those who commit acts of "cowardice, unkindness, and selfishness"; they could see a 90 percent increase in their taxes. Oh, and

to promote good taste and a more sophisticated sense of style among Britons, "houses with visible net curtains will be subject to a 5 percent increase in council tax charges and will not be eligible for any of the usual reductions." Posted on http://www.bbc.co.uk/bbcthree/tv/purple_party_manifesto2.shtml and accessed February 25, 2007. This page has since been removed.

6. Posted on http://www.nymag.com/news/politics/16713/ and accessed March 17, 2007.

7. Ibid.

8. You can find the results of the poll at http://www.rasmussenreports.com/ public_content/politics/mood_of_america/party_affiliation/number_of_ republicans_in_u_s_hits_new_low_number_of_democrats_also_decline. Accessed November 3, 2007.

9. On second thought, maybe we should. It would be fun to watch the ensuing indictments race through the courts.

10. Thanks to Jackie Salit of CUIP for articulating this.

11. Remember? In a 1999 interview with CNN's Wolf Blitzer, Gore, who was then vice president, said that while in Congress, he "took the initiative in creating the Internet." And then he took a whole lot of flak for claiming that. Posted on http://www.cnn.com/ALLPOLITICS/stories/1999/03/09/president.2000/transcript.gore/ and accessed June 17, 2007.

12. "This" meaning the ill will we've brought upon ourselves globally and the failure to provide for ourselves domestically (think Katrina, more than *three years* later).

13. David Lesher with Mark Baldassare, "Declining to State: Why Are Fewer California Voters Declaring Support for a Major Political Party?" *Press-Enterprise,* April 8, 2006. Posted on http://www.newamerica.net/publications/ articles/2006/declining_to_state and accessed March 20 and June 30, 2007.

14. Stuart Steers, "The Power of Purple: More Unaffiliated Suburbanites Vote 'for the Person'—Not the Red or Blue," *Rocky Mountain News,* September 23, 2006. Posted on http://www.insidedenver.com/drmn/elections/article/ 0,2808,DRMN_24736_5015623,00.html and accessed March 23 and June 29, 2007.

15. Kim Zetter, "Florida E-Vote Fraud? Unlikely," November 10, 2004. Posted on http://www.wired.com/politics/security/news/2004/11/ 65665?currentPage=all and accessed June 30, 2007.

16. Rick Klein, "Independents Rule New Hampshire: Partyless, Unpredictable Voters Could Sway Primary . . . Again." June 4, 2007. Posted on http://www. abcnews.go.com/Politics/story?id=3242844&page=1 and accessed June 28, 2007.

17. Posted on http://www.paindependents.org/Independent_PA_Info/PA_ Facts_and_Figures/54/ and accessed June 15, 2007.

18. John J. DiIulio Jr., "You Gotta Be Purple to Win: How the Democrats Did It," November 20, 2006. Posted on http://www.weeklystandard.com/Utilities/printer_preview.asp?idArticle=12956&R=EEC251A5 and accessed March 23, 2007.

19. Ibid.

20. Thomas Kostigen, "All Politics Is Local and Green Politics Are No Exception." Posted on http://www.alternet.org/environment/54915/ and accessed July 10, 2007.

21. I need to remind that last group that I am definitely a senior.

22. He's not kidding. Former mayor Joseph Santopietro served six years for bank fraud, bribery, embezzling federal funds, and tax evasion. Former mayor Phillip Giordano is serving a thirty-seven-year sentence for sexual crimes against minors that allegedly took place in the mayor's office. He was being investigated for municipal corruption when FBI agents discovered evidence of the sex crimes. While he was in prison, he tried to collect $61,000 in back pay from the city of Waterbury.

CHAPTER 2: CHANGING AMERICA

1. If you don't believe me, check out the C-SPAN coverage of the at-times hilarious panel discussion. It's not available to view online, but if you're really, really interested in all this, you can order the DVD "Voting for Independents" from www.c-span.org. The direct link is http://www.c-spanarchives.org/library/index.php?main_page-product_video_info&products_id-196456-1&highlight-independents. Should that link change, the best way to find the product is to search by the date the event was held (January 28, 2007) or aired (February 7, 2007). By the time you read this, though, copies may be available through interlibrary loan or possibly on eBay.

2. I later discovered that in 1992 the U.S. Supreme Court ruled that voters did not have the right to a write-in option. Blank ballots, in which every candidate was essentially a "write-in," were at one time the norm in the United States.

3. Ballot-access legislation changes, or is challenged, frequently. A number of significant efforts were being made to change Georgia law at the time of this writing. The petition requirements may have changed since the summer of 2007—but not necessarily for the better.

4. Posted on http://www.ga.lp.org/bibb/VoterChoice.html and last accessed June 20, 2007.

5. A Libertarian candidate qualified for the ballot in a special congressional election to fill a vacancy in June 2007, but the petitioning requirement did not apply in that case.

6. Winger believes reforming the electoral college will solve the ballot-access

problem: "When they change the electoral college, they'll have to federalize the whole ballot access procedure for president. . . . They'll have to have uniform rules for the whole country for the presidential race."

7. Thomas E. Patterson, *The Vanishing Voter: Public Involvement in an Age of Uncertainty* (New York: Alfred A. Knopf, 2002), 139.

8. Ann DeLaney, *Politics for Dummies* (Foster City, Calif.: IDG Books, 1995), 288.

9. So maybe they didn't use the word *bizarre,* but according to the National Archives Web site, legislators have introduced more than seven hundred proposals over the past two hundred years to reform or abolish the electoral college. "There have been more proposals for Constitutional amendments on changing the Electoral College than on any other subject. . . . Public opinion polls have shown Americans favored abolishing it by majorities of 58 percent in 1967; 81 percent in 1968; and 75 percent in 1981." The site briefly explains independents' distaste for the system: "Third parties have not fared well in the Electoral College system. . . . The last third party or splinter party candidate to make a strong showing was Theodore Roosevelt in 1912 (Progressive, also known as the Bull Moose Party). He finished a distant second in electoral and popular votes (taking 88 of the 266 electoral votes needed to win). Although Ross Perot won 19 percent of the popular vote nationwide in 1992, he did not win any electoral votes since he was not particularly strong in any one [state] or several states." Posted on http://www.archives.gov/federal-register/electoral-college/faq.html and last accessed June 21, 2007.

10. Maine and Nebraska both split their electoral votes according to congressional districts.

11. Mark Satin, *Radical Middle: The Politics We Need Now* (Boulder, Colo.: Westview Press, 2004).

12. That 1995 decision denied states the right to impose term limits on their congressional delegations.

13. Posted on http://www.cato.org/pubs/handbook/hb105-5.html and accessed July 6, 2007.

14. See http://www.termlimits.com for their effort, based on 2 Chronicles 7:14: "If my people, who are called by my name, will humble themselves and pray and seek my face and turn from their wicked ways, then will I hear from heaven and will forgive their sin and will heal their land" (NIV).

15. Posted on http://www.pacleansweep.com/founder.html and accessed July 6, 2007.

16. Posted by the elusive Eli on http://www.firedoglake.com/2007/03/06/who-wants-to-be-a-candidate and accessed March 18, 2007.

17. For those who need a refresher, in 1971 Ellsberg, a military analyst for

the defense department, leaked a top-secret report on the Vietnam War to a *New York Times* reporter. The document, which didn't exactly make President Johnson or the defense department look good, became known as the Pentagon Papers; among other things, the seven-thousand-page report proved that the government knew early on that the war was unwinnable and that casualties would be much higher than publicly stated.

18. I made up the fondling and flourishing part.

19. I couldn't find a reputable enough source for Stuart's role in this story, so I'm alleging it.

20. Author interview, May 2007.

CHAPTER 3: CHANGING AMERICA—PART 2

1. For those of you under a certain age, McGovern's only electoral votes came from Massachusetts (and the District of Columbia). Yep, it was a rout. A landslide. A trouncing.

2. "The New Face of Jim Crow: Voter Suppression in America," People For the American Way. Posted on http://www.pfaw.org/pfaw/general/default. aspx?oid=22222 and accessed April 12, 2007. People For the American Way is a clearly one-sided organization that takes on the radical right/religious right every chance it gets, but this report is worth reading regardless of your political persuasion—as long as you bear in mind that both parties engage in question-able practices.

3. Don't even think of arguing with me about this. I'm nothing if not a stodgy logophile.

4. Posted on http://www.nnseek.com/e/alt.politics.elections/option_to_regis-ter_independent_taken_off_from_the_arizona_9696808t.html and accessed July 1, 2007.

5. Posted on http://www.fairvote.org/?page=1801 and accessed June 12, 2007.

6. Posted on http://www.sfgate.com/cgi-bin/article.cgi?f=/c/a/2007/03/07/BAGNTOGLT81.DTL&feed=rss.bayarea and accessed April 10, 2007.

7. Posted on http://www.brennancenter.org/subpage.asp?key=38&init_key=9153 and accessed July 9, 2007.

8. Posted on http://www.tompaine.com/articles/2007/03/28/whose_elec-tion_fraud.php and accessed May 12, 2007.

9. Thomas E. Patterson, *The Vanishing Voter: Public Involvement in an Age of Uncertainty* (New York: Alfred A. Knopf, 2002), 133.

10. The chart is posted on http://www.eac.gov/voter/Register_to_Vote/deadlines/?searchterm=voter_registration_deadlines. Accessed November 2, 2007.

11. Patterson, *The Vanishing Voter*, 133.

12. Spencer Overton, *Stealing Democracy: The New Politics of Voter Suppression* (New York: W. W. Norton, 2006), 157.

13. Posted on http://www.independentvoting.org and accessed March 23, 2007.

14. Patterson, *The Vanishing Voter,* 82.

15. Because Election Day and many primaries fall during the school year, college students who register to vote in their schools' jurisdictions sometimes find that their rights are challenged by election boards that fail to recognize them as full-time residents.

16. Misapplication of voting-rights laws is a bigger deal than it would appear to be, especially when laws are applied inconsistently and along racial lines. Inmates who were convicted of so-called "black crimes" are less likely to have their voting rights reinstated or to be told those rights have already been reinstated.

17. Posted on http://www.statesman.com/opinion/content/editorial/stories/05/24/24gallegos_edit.html and accessed June 12, 2007. The page has since been removed.

CHAPTER 4: UNDECIDED? I THINK NOT

1. Joe Garcia, "There Is a New Party in the State: Independents," *The Arizona Republic,* May 20, 2007. Posted on http://www.azcentral.com/arizonarepublic/viewpoints/articles/0520garcia0520.html and accessed May 31, 2007.

2. Mark Gersh, "Swing Voters," *Blueprint* magazine, July 25, 2004. Posted on http://www.ppionline.org/ndol/print.cfm?contentid=252802 and accessed April 5, 2007.

3. Ibid.

4. I can't remember where I heard him say that—probably on the radio—but I'm using this opportunity to encourage you to read his book *Do I Stand Alone?* (New York: Pocket Books, 2001). Whatever your opinion of him, that book is a worthwhile read.

5. Mark J. Penn, "Swing Is Still King at the Polls," *Washington Post,* March 21, 2006, A17. Posted on http://www.washingtonpost.com/wp-dyn/content/article/2006/03/20/AR2006032001415_pf.html and accessed April 30, 2007.

6. Jacqueline Salit, "Can Independents Add Sway to Their Swing?" First published as "Newly Empowered Independents Want to Add Sway to Their Swing" in the *Worcester Telegram Gazette*, January 19, 2007. Posted on http://www.independentvoting.org/CanIndependentsAddSwaytoTheirSwing.html. Accessed November 2, 2007.

7. Ibid.

CHAPTER 5: THE ONLINE ELECTORATE

1. On a totally unrelated topic, the Web site www.stumbleupon.com is great fun.

2. Jerome Armstrong and Markos Moulitsas, *Crashing the Gate: Netroots, Grassroots, and the Rise of People-Powered Politics* (White River Junction, VT: Chelsea Green Publishing Company, 2006), 2–3.

3. Technically, according to language authority William Safire, the earliest use of the word occurred on a University of California e-mail list in 1993, but the word didn't catch on until 2004 when Armstrong—unaware of the previous appearance of the word—used it in a blog entry about Howard Dean's campaign.

4. Gail Russell Chaddock, "Their Clout Rising, Blogs Are Courted by Washington's Elite," *Christian Science Monitor* (27 October 2005).

5. Allen used the term *macaca*—a word meaning "monkey" that is considered a slur in some African nations—in referring to a Webb campaign worker of Indian descent. The video is on YouTube.com, along with one showing the over-the-top reaction of Allen campaign workers in Charlottesville.

6. Daniel K. Glover, "The Rise of Blogs." Posted on http://www.beltwayblogroll.nationaljournal.com/archives/2006/01/the_rise_of_blo.php on January 20, 2006 and accessed April 12, 2007.

7. Jerome Armstrong and Markos Moulitsas, *Crashing the Gate: Netroots, Grassroots, and the Rise of People-Powered Politics* (White River Junction, VT: Chelsea Green Publishing Company, 2006), 173.

8. Since you asked: www.marciaford.com, http://wethepurple.blogspot.com, http://postmodernmisfit.blogspot.com/, and http://myspace.com/wethepurple.

9. Lee Rainie and John Horrigan, "The Internet Is Creating a New Class of Web-Savvy Political Activists," Pew Research Center. Posted on http://www.pewresearch.org/pubs/280/election-2006-online on January 17, 2007 and accessed March 23, 2007.

10. John B. Horrigan, "Politics in Cyberspace: As Mid-Term Elections Loom, a Record Number of Americans Look to the Net for Information and Guidance." Posted on http://www.pewresearch.org/pubs/65/politics-in-cyberspace on September 20, 2006 and accessed May 14, 2007.

11. Michael Cornfield and Lee Rainie. "The Internet and Politics: No Revolution, Yet." Posted on http://www.pewresearch.org/pubs/85/the-internet-and-politics-no-revolution-yet on November 6, 2006 and accessed April 5, 2007.

12. Supposedly an apathetic bunch, but then they didn't have monolithic rallying points like Vietnam, 9/11, and Iraq. They're forgiven.

13. Voting-Age Population, Percent Reporting Registered, and Voted: 1992 to 2004. Table 405. *Statistical Abstract of the United States: 2007.* Posted on

http://www.census.gov/prod/2006pubs/07statab/election.pdf and accessed July 12, 2007.

14. Mike Connery, "Case Studies in Young Voter Mobilization." Posted on http://www.mydd.com/story/2007/6/8/12544/15428 on June 8, 2007 and accessed June 9, 2007.

15. Mike Connery, "Deconstructing Progressive Youth Activism." Posted on http://mydd.com/story/2007/6/3/21642/42438 on June 3, 2007 and accessed June 3, 2007.

16. Connery, "Case Studies in Young Voter Mobilization."

17. Susan Milligan, "Youth Voters a Force in '08 Race." Posted on http://www.boston.com/news/nation/articles/2007/05/13/youth_voters_a_force_in_08_race?mode=PF on May 13, 2007 and accessed May 27, 2007.

18. "New Online Database Documents Resurgence of Progressive Faith Organizing." Posted on http://www.faithinpubliclife.org/content/press/2007/06/new_online_database_documents_1.html on June 21, 2007 and accessed on June 25, 2007.

CHAPTER 6: THE PEW DISTRUST

1. Gregory A. Boyd, *The Myth of a Christian Nation: How the Quest for Political Power is Destroying the Church* (Grand Rapids: Zondervan, 2006), 143.
2. Boyd adheres to a controversial doctrine known as "open theism," which some evangelicals consider heretical as it seems to deny God's omniscience. Boyd affirms God's omniscience and provides a better understanding of his views in the Q&A section of his ministry's Web site, http://www.christusvictorministries.org. In any event, this doctrinal view is unrelated to his views on the unhealthy relationship between the church and partisan politics.
3. The Church of God in Christ, the largest Pentecostal denomination in the world and one of the largest African-American denominations. It's been a while since I've attended a COGIC service. At the time, I was immersed in the charismatic/Pentecostal world, but my feeble outbursts paled amid the congregation's shouts of agreement during the services.
4. For the record, 67 percent of Americans disagree with Boyd and me about this, according to a 2006 report from the Pew Forum on Religion and Public Life.
5. Obery M. Hendricks Jr., *The Politics of Jesus: Rediscovering the True Revolutionary Nature of Jesus' Teachings and How They Have Been Corrupted* (New York: Doubleday, 2006), 281.
6. Jerry Filteau, "Cardinal McCarrick Warns against Partisan Politics within Church." Posted on http://www.catholicnews.com/data/stories/cns/0603512.htm and accessed July 12, 2007.
7. It's in the Bible. See Psalm 137:9.

8. "John D. Roth Responds," *Mennonite Life,* June 2005. Posted on http://www.bethelks.edu/mennonitelife/2005June/roth.php and accessed July 15, 2007.

9. Posted on http://www.ajc.com/opinion/content/opinion/stories/2007/05/16/0517edfalwell.html and accessed July 4, 2007.

10. Posted on http://www.crosswalk.com/blogs/dean/11536056/ and accessed April 3, 2007.

11. For a fascinating look at the GOP's attitude toward evangelicals, David Kuo's *Tempting Faith* (New York: Free Press, 2006) is as good as it gets.

12. Some fundamentalist churches believe that the only accurate Bible translation is the King James, which I discovered back in the 1970s when I carried my New American Standard Bible into a service at an unfamiliar church and was indirectly reprimanded from the pulpit. I never did *that* again.

13. Tony Campolo, "Using the Church for Partisan Politics." Posted on http://www.huffingtonpost.com/tony-campolo/using-the-church-for-part_b_48046.html and accessed June 7, 2007.

14. Ibid.

15. Florida evangelist Bill Keller attracted the attention of Americans United for Separation of Church and State, and consequently the IRS, with a Web site post warning his 2.4 million subscribers, "If you vote for Mitt Romney, you are voting for Satan!" Which poses these larger questions: *Bill Keller has* 2.4 million *subscribers? You're kidding, right?*

16. Dan Gilgoff, "Turning a Blind Eye, IRS Enables Church Politicking." Posted on http://blogs.usatoday.com/oped/2007/01/turning_a_blind.html and accessed May 13, 2007.

17. Bob Edgar, *Middle Church: Reclaiming the Moral Values of the Faithful Majority from the Religious Right* (New York: Simon & Schuster, 2006), 169.

18. Ibid., 218.

19. Americans United for Separation of Church and State, "Religion, Partisan Politics and Tax Exemption: What Federal Law Requires and Why." Brochure posted on http://www.projectfairplay.org/brochure/ and accessed May 20, 2007.

20. Posted on http://www.redeemthevote.com/rtvnews212.html and accessed July 22, 2007.

21. Dan Gilgoff, *The Jesus Machine: How James Dobson, Focus on the Family, and Evangelical America Are Winning the Culture War* (New York: St. Martin's Press, 2007).

22. I used to be the editor of *Christian Retailing,* which was and is a great trade magazine, though there's something disquieting about the whole idea of "Christian retailing."

23. Laurie Goodstein, "Disowning Conservative Politics, Evangelical Pastor

Rattles Flock," *New York Times,* July 30, 2006. Posted on http://www.nytimes.com/2006/07/30/us/30pastor.html?ex=1311912000&en=28c82f6fb9327ad1&ei=5088 and accessed May 10, 2007.

24. Posted on http://www.abcnews.go.com/print?id=3138468 and accessed May 21, 2007.

25. Stanley Hauerwas and William H. Willimon, *Resident Aliens: Life in the Christian Colony* (Nashville: Abingdon Press, 1989), 47.

26. Portions of this article originally appeared on the Web site Explorefaith.org in an essay titled "The Emerging Church: Ancient Faith for a Postmodern World" by Marcia Ford.

CHAPTER 7: OUR TWO-ISSUE SYSTEM

1. Back in the 1970s, the issue was gay rights in general. The right to marry is just about the last of the rights they've been denied.

2. National Abortion Rights Action League.

3. Posted on http://www.moodymagazine.com/articles.php?action=view_article&id=549 and accessed June 23, 2007. Hird's article also pointed out that Christian women who have abortions are at a higher risk for emotional distress because of the guilt they experience.

4. Melinda Henneberger, *If They Only Listened to Us: What Women Voters Want Politicians to Hear* (New York: Simon & Schuster, 2007), 9.

5. Ibid.,137.

6. David Kuo, *Tempting Faith: An Inside Story of Political Seduction* (New York: Free Press, 2006), 25.

7. Henneberger, *If They Only Listened to Us,* 88.

8. Melinda Henneberger, "Why Pro-Choice Is a Bad Choice for Democrats," *New York Times,* June 22, 2007. Posted on http://www.nytimes.com/2007/06/22/opinion/22henneberger.html?ei=5124&en=df9f45ebdbbe2c9b&ex=1340164800&partner=permalink&exprod=permalink&pagewanted=print and accessed June 30, 2007.

9. His April 12, 2007 appearance was a hoot. You can view it at http://www.comedycentral.com/motherload/player.jhtml?ml_video=85184&ml_collection=&ml_gateway=&ml_gateway_id=&ml_comedian=&ml_runtime=&ml_context=show&ml_origin_url=/shows/the_colbert_report/videos/celebrity_interviews/index.jhtml%3FplayVideo%3D85184&ml_playlist=&lnk=&is_large=true. Oh, forget it. Just go to www.comedycentral.com and search for "Richard Land."

10. Richard Land, *The Divided States of America? What Liberals and Conservatives Are Missing in the God-and-Country Shouting Match!* (Nashville: Thomas Nelson, 2007), 192.

11. Pietro S. Nivola, ed. *Red and Blue Nation? Characteristics and Causes of America's Polarized Politics.* (Washington: Brookings Institution Press, 2006). From the essay "Polarized by God?" by E. J. Dionne Jr., 183.

12. Ibid., 205.

13. A Christian abstinence program.

14. Posted on http://www.abcnews.go.com/print?id=3138468 and accessed May 30, 2007.

15. Nivola, *Red and Blue Nation?* 183.

16. Land, *The Divided States of America?* 24.

17. Obviously, this method of "lawmaking" applies to other issues as well. Savvy proponents of all manner of public policy issues have figured out that you'll get quicker action in our clogged court system than you will in Congress.

CHAPTER 8: FINAL TALLY

1. Posted on http://www.democracycampaign.org/purpose.html and accessed May 25, 2007.

2. Posted on http://college.unity08.com/about and accessed November 3, 2007.

3. Author interview, August 2007.

Glossary of Sorts

527: A tax-exempt organization that attempts to influence elections by advocating for specific issues and by mobilizing people to vote; think the conservative group Swift Boat Veterans for Truth, which called into question John Kerry's military service in the 2004 presidential election, and an arm of the liberal group MoveOn.org that focuses on voter registration and education. Because money from 527s is not used to directly support a particular candidate, these groups are able to circumvent Federal Election Commission regulations.

Approval voting: Largely designed for local elections, this is a method of voting in which voters place a check mark by each candidate they approve. The candidate with the highest number of check marks wins.

Ballot access: The determination of whose names will appear on the ballot for local, state, and federal elections. Ballot access laws vary widely, and often wildly, from one jurisdiction to another. I'm guessing that because the two major parties dominate the legislative bodies that enact ballot-access laws, regulations that apply to independent and third-party candidates are nearly impossible to follow. But maybe that's a coincidence.

Campaign finance reform: An effort to reduce the amount of money spent on political campaigns and change the methods by which candidates receive funding. Current efforts include one that advocates providing a set amount of public funding for candidates who agree not to accept private donations and another that proposes allowing anonymous donations to be filtered through the Federal Election Commission.

Centrist: Can I avoid this one, please? Because no matter how I define this term and all the other political-persuasion terms in this section, *someone* will take me to task for it. Let's just say that you're probably a centrist if your fellow liberals think you're too conservative or your fellow conservatives think you're too liberal.

Citizen's congress: This term is used in other contexts, but with regard to U.S. politics, it refers to the notion that imposing term limits on our legislators would breathe new life into Congress, do away with the position of "career politician," and attract candidates from more walks of life than we see today.

Conservative: Generally, a political philosophy that advocates adherence to tradition, gradual change when change is necessary, fiscal restraint, and limited government intrusion into the lives of citizens. Ideally, that is. The main point I want to make here is that political conservatives and religious conservatives are not one and the same, though there's admittedly a lot of overlap. But it's entirely possible to be politically liberal and religiously conservative—that is, identifying with the liberal perspective on issues like war while maintaining what is considered to be a conservative perspective on, say, the Bible and the basics of the faith (here I am specifically referring to the Christian faith). I can provide names if you don't believe me.

Diebold machines: Electronic touch-screen voting machines that have been plagued with problems in accurately recording votes. An independent study at Princeton University verified the machines' vulnerability to hackers, and now "how to hack into a Diebold" instructions are all over the Internet.

Electoral college: You're kidding, right? You think I'd actually try to define this?

Fusion: In U.S. politics—and in a limited number of states—a structure through which a candidate can enjoy the support of more than one political party. The best-known example in recent years was Michael Bloomberg's run for mayor of New York City as both a Republican Party and Independence Party candidate.

Gerrymandering: See *redistricting*.

Hard money: Not to be confused with the clinking change in your pocket, hard money is that which is given directly to a candidate's campaign by an individual or a political action committee (see *PAC*). Hard-money contributions must meet stringent Federal Election Commission regulations.

Independent: An incredibly intelligent person who thinks for herself and has decided that neither major political party in the U.S. represents her political perspective. Okay, on a more objective note, a person who declines to register to vote as a Republican or Democrat. Politically active independents exist along the entire ideological spectrum but generally agree on the need for political reform.

Instant runoff voting: A method of voting by which voters rank candidates in order of their preference. The candidate who receives the highest amount of number-one votes wins.

Liberal: Political ideology that in the U.S. is generally associated with personal freedom issues, government-run social programs, equal opportunity, and so forth. Like conservatism, when you define liberalism in such terms, you can get the impression that the two ideologies aren't all that far apart. But when you get down to defining details—such as, say, *specific* personal freedoms—well, the differences become apparent.

Libertarian: With a capital *L,* a member of the Libertarian Party. Lowercase libertarians may or may not agree with the positions of the Libertarian Party, but the capitals and lowercases all agree on this point: Each individual has absolute authority, control, and sovereignty over his own life, body, and personal property. So there. Please, *please,* don't confuse libertarians with libertines, who take personal freedom to a whole different level and into a whole different arena.

Minor party: See *third party.*

Moderate: A politically moderate person holds liberal views on some issues and conservative views on others and generally tries to reconcile the two perspectives.

National popular vote plan: A proposal that encourages states to enter into a compact to assign their electoral votes to the presidential candidate who gets the most actual votes. If for no other reason, this plan should be enacted as a way to circumvent the bizarre institution known as the electoral college.

Nonpartisan election: Local elections in which candidates do not run in affiliation with a particular political party. In some cases—particularly elections in larger cities—it's fairly obvious to which party the candidate belongs; in other contests, the candidate's party is less relevant and often unknown.

Open primary: A primary election in which anyone can vote, regardless of the individual's party affiliation. In most open primaries, voters simply choose either the Republican or Democratic ballot (voters, of course, can only fill out one party's ballot; don't think you can vote in both parties' contests).

PAC: A political action committee is a group that's organized to support a specific candidate (or piece of legislation). PACs are highly regulated, or so they say. Two examples of groups whose PACs work diligently to influence elections are the National Education Association and the National Rifle Association.

Poll tax: A tax that was charged to blacks, Native Americans, and certain whites following the Civil War, for the privilege of voting. Because members of those groups were nearly all poor, the tax served to disenfranchise them. Some consider requiring prospective voters to pay for government-issued I.D. cards to be a form of poll tax.

Populist: One who is a strong advocate of personal liberty, especially as defined by the Bill of Rights and just as strong an opponent of military aggression. Supports a decentralized government that is both open and accountable to the people.

Progressive: A political ideology that seeks to move society forward by advocating for economic, racial, and social justice and equality—and to make government more responsive to the will of the people.

Radical: A term traditionally used to define the extreme wings of far-right conservatism and far-left liberalism but that now includes the "radical middle" or "radical centrists."

Rank-order voting: See *instant runoff voting.*

Reactionary: Highly pejorative term usually referring to ultra-, mega-, radical conservatives.

Redistricting: Changing the boundaries of a congressional district. Gerrymandering refers to reconfiguring a district in such a way that it clearly favors one political party over another.

Same-day voter registration: Self-defining, but many people can't believe that it actually means what it says, so here goes: the ability to register to vote on Election Day so you can vote in the actual election being held that very day.

Soft money: Contributions given to a political party that cannot be used in direct support of a candidate. Soft money can be used to advocate support for the party's position on specific issues. Not to be confused with the dwindling number of paper bills in your wallet.

Swing voter: Technically, a voter whose vote swings from one party to another, from one election to another—but most often between the two major political parties.

Term limits: See *citizen's congress.*

Third party: Any political party that is not one of the two major parties in the U.S. Among the largest are the Green Party, the Libertarian Party, and the Constitution Party.

Web Sites of Interest to Independents

It would be impossible to list all the worthwhile independent-voter blogs and Web sites I've discovered, so I've pared the list down to sites that reflect general interests. Some of the links below refer to sites mentioned in the previous chapters, but some referred to earlier are not on the list below. That is no reflection on their value to independent voters but rather an effort to avoid too much duplication. Be sure to visit the sites mentioned in the chapters as well.

Most of the sites below provide a list of links to sites that narrow the field to, say, independent conservatives, evangelical progressives, or liberal populists.

Ballot Access News (http://www.ballot-access.org/): This one's a real eye-opener, even if you're not interested in ballot-access issues. Just read a few random posts, and you'll get an inkling of the challenges faced by independent candidates—and independent voters trying to simply register as independents. Of course, if you're a ballot-access junkie, this is where you'll get your fix.

Central Sanity (http://www.centralsanity.blogspot.com/): "Supporting the Rebellion of Reasonable People in an Unreasonable World." This site is for moderate Republican and independent voters but provides news and smart commentary that transcends political ideology.

Committee for a Unified Independent Party (CUIP) (http://www.independentvoting. org/index.html): Pretty much a national clearinghouse for all things politically independent. This group has done more to rally and unite independents than any organization or individual out there. Great source of information and news, plus a link to the CUIP publication *The Neo-Independent,* where you'll find indie-related articles and commentary. This is where you start if you want to find out more or connect with other independents nationwide.

The Hankster (http://grassrootsindependent.blogspot.com/): Hands down, the best source for daily political news that independents would be interested in.

Nancy Hanks has been politically active for decades and really knows her stuff. It would be a good idea to bookmark her site and visit it often.

Independent Texans (http://www.indytexans.org/): Lots of information of interest to Texans, but also some great information on political reform; just follow the link by that name in the left column.

Independent Voice (http://www.independentvoice.org/): The voice of California's 3.6 million independents, or at least those who have found the site and appreciate its perspective on independent politics. There's lots of overlap here with CUIP, but it's still a site worth visiting.

The Moderate Voice (http://www.themoderatevoice.com/): "Domestic and international news analysis, irreverent comments, original reporting, and popular culture features from across the political spectrum." Sometimes just fun stuff, but often the kind of news you won't get from the mainstream media. Well worth checking out.

Project Vote Smart (http://votesmart.org/index.htm): An all-around excellent site for information on candidates and the issues. Besides, you have to love a group that boasts a purple bus and the slogan, "We provide more information about the candidates than they remember about themselves."

The Purple State (http://thepurplestate.com/): "Political Commentary from the Youth Vote"; specifically, a group of students, mostly from Vassar, who founded the site because they "could not take it anymore"—"it" being the partisanship that is obscuring the nation's real concerns. Now they're blogging, and what they have to say is significant.

WatchBlog (http://watchblog.com/): I especially like the format of this site, which provides three columns of news and commentary of interest to Democrats and liberals, third-party voters and independents, and Republicans and conservatives. After reading the items in the center column, dedicated to us, you can spy on the partisans to the left and right.

★

Bibliography and Recommended Reading

Armstrong, Jerome and Markos Moulitsas. *Crashing the Gate: Netroots, Grassroots, and the Rise of People-Powered Politics.* White River Junction, VT: Chelsea Green Publishing Company, 2006.

Balmer, Randall. *Thy Kingdom Come: How the Religious Right Distorts the Faith and Threatens America.* New York: Basic Books, 2006.

Danforth, John. *Faith and Politics: How the "Moral Values" Debate Divides America and How to Move Forward Together.* New York: Viking Penguin, 2006.

Dionne, E. J. Jr., ed. *One Electorate under God? A Dialogue on Religion and American Politics.* Washington: Brookings Institution Press, 2004.

Edgar, Bob. *Middle Church: Reclaiming the Moral Values of the Faithful Majority from the Religious Right.* New York: Simon & Schuster, 2006.

Gilgoff, Dan. *The Jesus Machine: How James Dobson, Focus on the Family, and Evangelical America Are Winning the Culture War.* New York: St. Martin's Press, 2007.

Goldberg, Michelle. *Kingdom Coming: The Rise of Christian Nationalism.* New York: W.W. Norton, 2006.

Halperin, Mark, and John F. Harris. *The Way to Win: Taking the White House in 2008.* New York: Random House, 2006.

Halstead, Ted and Michael Lind. *The Radical Center: The Future of American Politics.* New York: Doubleday, 2001.

Hamburger, Tom and Peter Wallsten. *One Party Country: The Republican Plan for Dominance in the 21st Century.* Hoboken, NJ: John Wiley & Sons, 2006.

Hauerwas, Stanley and William H. Willimon. *Resident Aliens: Life in the Christian Colony*. Nashville: Abingdon Press, 1989.

Hendricks, Obery M. Jr. *The Politics of Jesus: Rediscovering the True Revolutionary Nature of Jesus' Teachings and How They Have Been Corrupted*. New York: Doubleday, 2006.

Henneberger, Melinda. *If They Only Listened to Us: What Women Voters Want Politicians to Hear*. New York: Simon & Schuster, 2007.

Hollenbach, David. *The Global Face of Public Faith: Politics, Human Rights, and Christian Ethics*. Washington: Georgetown University Press, 2003.

Horowitz, David. *The Politics of Bad Faith: The Radical Assault on America's Future*. New York: Free Press, 1998.

Keith, Bruce E., David B. Magleby, Candice J. Nelson, Elizabeth Orr, Mark C. Westlye, and Raymond E. Wolfinger. *The Myth of the Independent Voter*. Berkeley, CA: University of California Press, 1992.

Kuo, David. *Tempting Faith: An Inside Story of Political Seduction*. New York: Free Press, 2006.

Land, Richard. *The Divided States of America? What Liberals and Conservatives Are Missing in the God-and-Country Shouting Match*. Nashville: Thomas Nelson, 2007.

Lowenstein, Daniel H. and Richard L. Hasen, eds. *Election Law Journal*, vol. 5, no. 2, 2006. New Rochelle, NY: Mary Ann Liebert, Inc.

Martin, William. *With God on Our Side: The Rise of the Religious Right in America*. New York: Broadway Books, 1996.

Matthews, Chris. *Hardball: How Politics Is Played, Told by One Who Knows the Game*. New York: Touchstone, 1999.

Miller, Matthew. *The Two Percent Solution: Fixing America's Problems in Ways Liberals and Conservatives Can Love*. New York: Public Affairs, 2003.

Nelson, James A. *Where Would Jesus Put the Sidewalks? A Study of Faith & Politics: A Most Holy Alliance*. Portland, OR: Inkwater Press, 2004.

Nivola, Pietro S., ed. *Red and Blue Nation? Characteristics and Causes of America's Polarized Politics*. Washington: Brookings Institution Press, 2006.

Overton, Spencer. *Stealing Democracy: The New Politics of Voter Suppression*. New York: W.W. Norton, 2006.

Patterson, Thomas E. *The Vanishing Voter: Public Involvement in an Age of Uncertainty*. New York: Alfred A. Knopf, 2002.

Press, Bill. *How the Republicans Stole Christmas: The Republican Party's Declared Monopoly on Religion and What Democrats Can Do to Take It Back*. New York: Doubleday, 2005.

Raschke, Carl, ed. *The Republic of Faith: The Search for Agreement amid Diversity in American Religion*. Aurora, CO: The Davies Group Publishers, 2005.

Reed, Ralph. *Politically Incorrect: The Emerging Faith Factor in American Politics*. Dallas: Word Publishing, 1994.

Reed, Ralph. *Active Faith: How Christians Are Changing the Soul of American Politics*. New York: Free Press, 1996.

Reichley, A. James. *Faith in Politics*. Washington: The Brookings Institution, 2002.

Satin, Mark. *Radical Middle: The Politics We Need Now*. Boulder, CO: Westview Press, 2004.

Suarez, Ray. *The Holy Vote: The Politics of Faith in America*. New York: HarperCollins, 2006.

Wallis, Jim. *The Soul of Politics: Beyond "Religious Right" and "Secular Left."* New York: Harvest, 1995.

Wallis, Jim. *God's Politics: Why the Right Gets It Wrong and the Left Doesn't Get It*. New York: HarperCollins, 2005.

Wattenberg, Martin P. *The Decline of American Political Parties, 1952-1996*. Cambridge, MA: Harvard University Press, 1998.

Wolfson, Lewis W. *The Untapped Power of the Press: Explaining Government to the People.* New York: Praeger Special Studies, 1985.

Wuthnow, Robert, ed. *The Quiet Hand of God: Faith-Based Activism and the Public Role of Mainline Protestantism.* Los Angeles: University of California Press, 2002.

★

About the Author

Marcia Ford, former editor of *Christian Retailing* magazine, is a contributor to *Publishers Weekly* and FaithfulReader.com. In addition to editing nearly one hundred books, she is the author of twenty books, including *Finding Hope, Traditions of the Ancients, The Sacred Art of Forgiveness, Memoir of a Misfit,* and with Scott Marshall, *Restless Pilgrim: The Spiritual Journey of Bob Dylan.* She has more than thirty years of experience in the publishing industry.

For more information, please visit www.marciaford.com or www.wethepurpleonline.com or e-mail misfit@marciaford.com.

★

Index